HAL LEONARD | BARITONE UKULELE CHORD FINDER

Over 1000 Ukulele Chords

ISBN 978-1-4234-8379-3

In Australia Contact
Hal Leonard Australia Pty. Ltd
4 Lentara Cour
Cheltenham, Victoria, 3192 Australia
Email: ausadmin@halleonard.com.au

Visit Hal Leonard Online a
www.halleonard.com

HAL•LEONARD®
CORPORATION

TABLE OF CONTENTS

Introduction 4

Chord Construction 5

    Triads 5

    Intervals 5

    7th Chords 6

    Extensions 6

    Inversions 7

Chord Qualities 8

Chords

    C 9

    D♭/C♯ 16

    D 23

    E♭/D♯ 30

    E 37

    F 44

    F♯/G♭ 51

    G 58

    A♭/G♯ 65

    A 72

    B♭/A♯ 79

    B 86

INTRODUCTION

Baritone Ukulele Chord Finder is an extensive reference guide to over 1,000 chords. Twenty-eight different chord qualities are covered for each key, and each chord quality is presented in three different voicings. Open strings are used when possible, but at least one voicing from each quality will be a moveable form. This allows for many unique voicings but also provides practical chord forms that can be transposed to any key. One thing to remember is that many of these moveable forms are also unique. So, just because you've learned two moveable shapes for C7, for example, that doesn't mean there aren't any more moveable seventh chord shapes in the book. Usually, you'll find other moveable voicings for the same chord by looking at other keys throughout the book.

A fingerboard chart of the entire ukulele neck through fret 12 is provided below for reference.

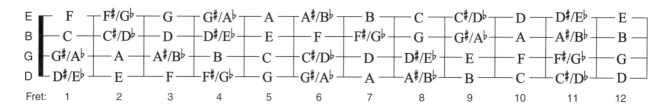

The chords throughout this book are presented in chord grid fashion. In case you're not familiar with this type of notation, below is a detailed explanation of how they're read.

The four vertical lines represent the strings on the ukulele.
The lowest string (D) is on the left, moving through to the highest string (E) on the right.

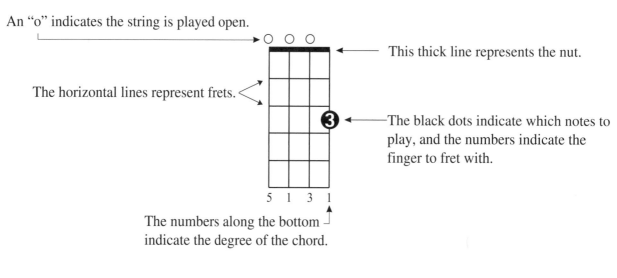

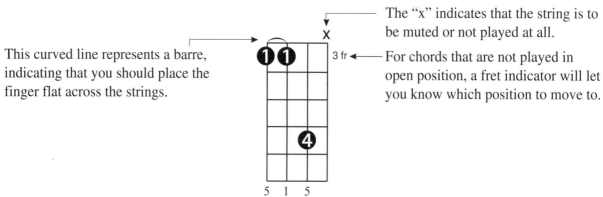

CHORD CONSTRUCTION

This section is intended to provide a basic knowledge of chords, how to build them, and how to use them. Some of you may already know this; if so, skip ahead! If not, read on and learn how to impress your friends who don't know.

TRIADS

A chord is simply a collection of notes deliberately arranged in a harmonious (or sometimes non-harmonious) fashion. The most common type of chord is called a *triad*. The name triad is telling of the number of notes in the chord—three. Triads can be one of four different qualities: major, minor, augmented, or diminished. Below, we find what's known as a C Major triad:

The words "root," "third," and "fifth" below the notes on the staff indicate how each note functions within the chord. A root note is the foundation of the chord and the note after which the chord will be named.

INTERVALS

The other two notes in our C triad (the 3rd and the 5th) are responsible for the *quality* of the chord. The notes C and E are an interval (or distance) of a major 3rd apart. Intervals are comprised of two components: a *number* and a *quality*.

In the case of the number, we can determine that C to E is a *3rd* by simply counting through the musical alphabet. Starting from C: C is one, D is two, and E is three. (The word "root" is many times used interchangeably with the number "1." For all practical purposes, they mean the same thing.) From C to G is a 5th, and we can confirm this by again counting up from C: C(1)–D(2)–E(3)–F(4)–G(5).

Determining the quality of an interval is not quite as easy as the number, but it's not too difficult. It will require a bit of memorization, but it's very logical. Below we'll find all twelve of the notes in the chromatic scale and their intervals measured from a C root note:

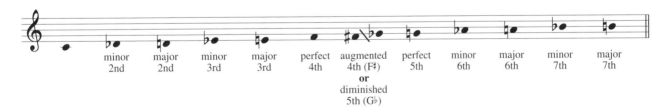

This example tells us a great deal about intervals. We can see a few formulas here at work. The first thing we should notice is that a minor interval is always one half step smaller than a major interval. C to E is a major 3rd, whereas C to E♭ is a minor 3rd. C to A is a major 6th, whereas C to A♭ is a minor 6th, etc. The next thing we should notice is how 4ths and 5ths work. We can see that an augmented interval is always one half step greater than a perfect one, and a diminished interval is always one half step smaller.

Any triad of one of the four above-mentioned qualities will contain a root, 3rd, and 5th. Other types of triads you may encounter include 6 chords, sus4 chords, and sus2 chords. These chords are the product of (in the case of sus4 and sus2 chords) replacing the 3rd with another note or (in the case of 6 chords) replacing the 5th (or sometimes adding to it) with another note.

Below are several different qualities of triads which will allow us to examine these intervals at work and note how they affect the names of these chords:

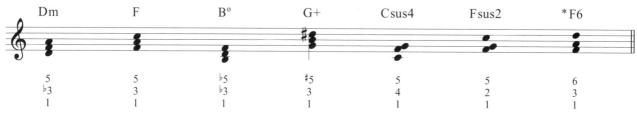

The symbol ∞ stands for diminished, while the symbol + stands for augmented.
* Note that the 5th tone may or may not be present in a 6 chord.

7TH CHORDS

Beyond the triad, we'll encounter many more chords, most commonly 7th chords. These chords will not only contain the root, 3rd, and 5th, but also the 7th. Below are a few common 7th chords. (Note that the 7th interval may be major or minor independent of the 3rd, thus affecting the name of the chord.)

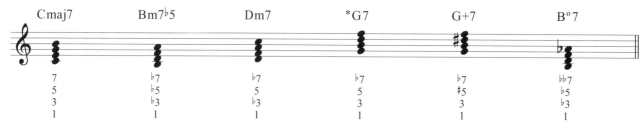

* Note that the G7 chord contains a major 3rd and a minor 7th. This type of chord is referred to as a *dominant 7th.*

EXTENSIONS

Finally, beyond 7th chords, we have extensions. The concept of extensions is a bit complicated and will only be touched upon here, as it requires more extensive study than is possible within the scope of this book. Basically, extended chords continue the process of stacking notes onto a triad that we began with the 7th chord. Instead of only adding the 7th to the chord, however, in a 9th chord we'll add the 7th and the 9th. In an 11th chord, we'll add the 7th, 9th, and 11th to our triad, etc. Now, here's the catch: not all of the notes need to be present in an extended chord. The general rule is, if the 7th is present, then notes other than the root, 3rd, and 5th are extensions and therefore numbered an octave higher (9, 11, 13). Since we're only capable of playing four notes at a time on the ukulele, we must decide which notes are important and which notes we can omit. Generally speaking, you'll want to include the root, 3rd, 7th, and the extension. The C13 chord below demonstrates this concept:

Note that there is no 5th (G) present in this chord, but the presence of the 7th (B♭) tells us that this chord is called C13, rather than some kind of C6 chord.

Extended chords may contain either the major 3rd or the perfect 11th, but usually not both. These two notes can clash with one another, since the 11th is equivalent to the 4th, only a half step away from the 3rd. In the C13 chord above, the 11th was omitted. In a chord where the 11th is specified, the major 3rd is usually omitted. There may be some cases where your ear tells you it is OK to use a chord with both notes. This book includes examples of both options, with emphasis on the common practice. Minor chords do not have this problem and may include the 11th and minor 3rd together.

INVERSIONS

Since the ukulele only has four strings, chords will often be voiced in *inversion*. A chord is inverted when a note other than the root is in the bass. In a triad, which contains three different notes, there are three basic possibilities for the vertical organization of the notes: root position, first inversion, and second inversion. Chords in root position contain the root of the chord in the bass; in other words, they are not inversions. A first inversion chord, however, contains the 3rd in the bass, while a second inversion chord contains the 5th in the bass. This is demonstrated below:

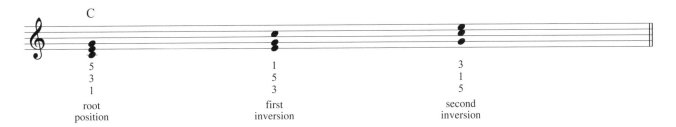

In a seventh chord or an extended chord, which contains four different notes, we have another inversion possibility. In addition to the first and second inversions, we can also have a third inversion, which places the 7th of the chord in the bass.

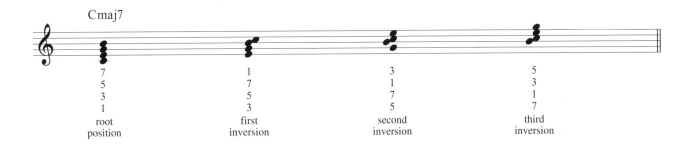

Occasionally, extended chords will feature an extension (9th, 11th, or 13th) in the bass. While these chords are inversions as well, they aren't typically numbered as with the triads and seventh chords. For instance, the chord below would most likely be called "D9 with E in the bass," or "D9 with the 9th in the bass," or simply "D9 over E."

Again, this section is intended to be a basic tutorial on the concept of chord construction and chord theory. If you're interested in furthering your knowledge on this subject, I suggest you take a look at some of the many books dedicated to chord construction and theory.

CHORD QUALITIES

Below is a list of the twenty-eight different chord qualities presented in this book, their abbreviations, and their formulas:

CHORD TYPE	ABBREVIATION	FORMULA
Major	C	1–3–5
Minor	Cm	1–♭3–5
Augmented	C+	1–3–♯5
Diminished	C°	1–♭3–♭5
Fifth (Power Chord)	C5	1–5
Added Ninth	Cadd9	1–3–5–9
Minor Added Ninth	Cm(add9)	1–♭3–5–9
Suspended Fourth	Csus4	1–4–5
Suspended Second	Csus2	1–2–5
Sixth	C6	1–3–5–6
Minor Sixth	Cm6	1–♭3–5–6
Major Seventh	Cmaj7	1–3–5–7
Major Ninth	Cmaj9	1–3–5–7–9
Minor Seventh	Cm7	1–♭3–5–♭7
Minor, Major Seventh	Cm(maj7)	1–♭3–5–7
Minor Seventh, Flat Fifth	Cm7♭5	1–♭3–♭5–♭7
Minor Ninth	Cm9	1–♭3–5–♭7–9
Minor Eleventh	Cm11	1–♭3–5–♭7–9–11
Seventh	C7	1–3–5–♭7
Seventh, Suspended Fourth	C7sus4	1–4–5–♭7
Augmented Seventh	C+7	1–3–♯5–♭7
Seventh, Flat Fifth	C7♭5	1–3–♭5–♭7
Ninth	C9	1–3–5–♭7–9
Seventh, Sharp Ninth	C7♯9	1–3–5–♭7–♯9
Seventh, Flat Ninth	C7♭9	1–3–5–♭7–♭9
Eleventh	C11	1–3–5–♭7–9–11*
Thirteenth	C13	1–3–5–♭7–9–11–13 **
Diminished Seventh	C°7	1–♭3–♭5–♭♭7

* The 3rd is sometimes omitted from an eleventh chord.
** The 11th is sometimes omitted from a thirteenth chord.

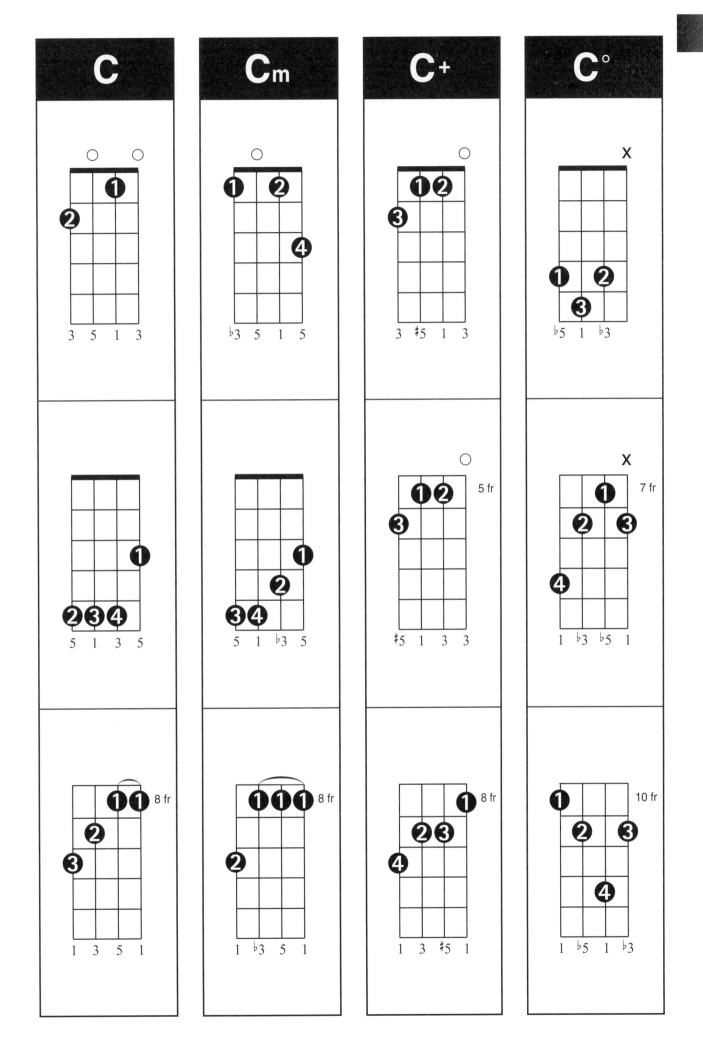

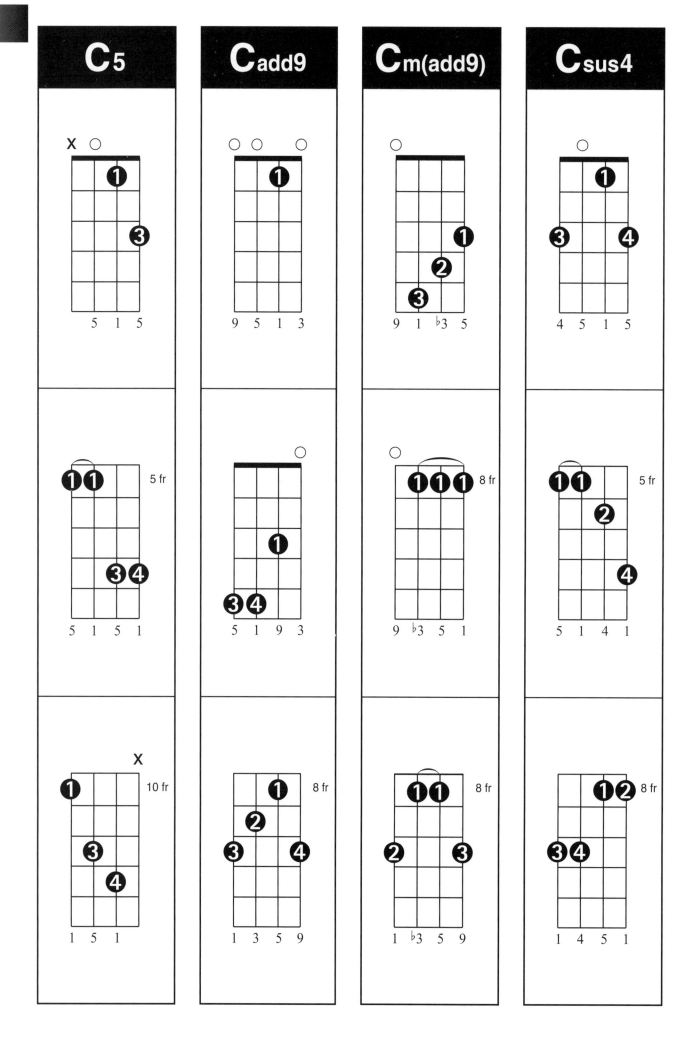

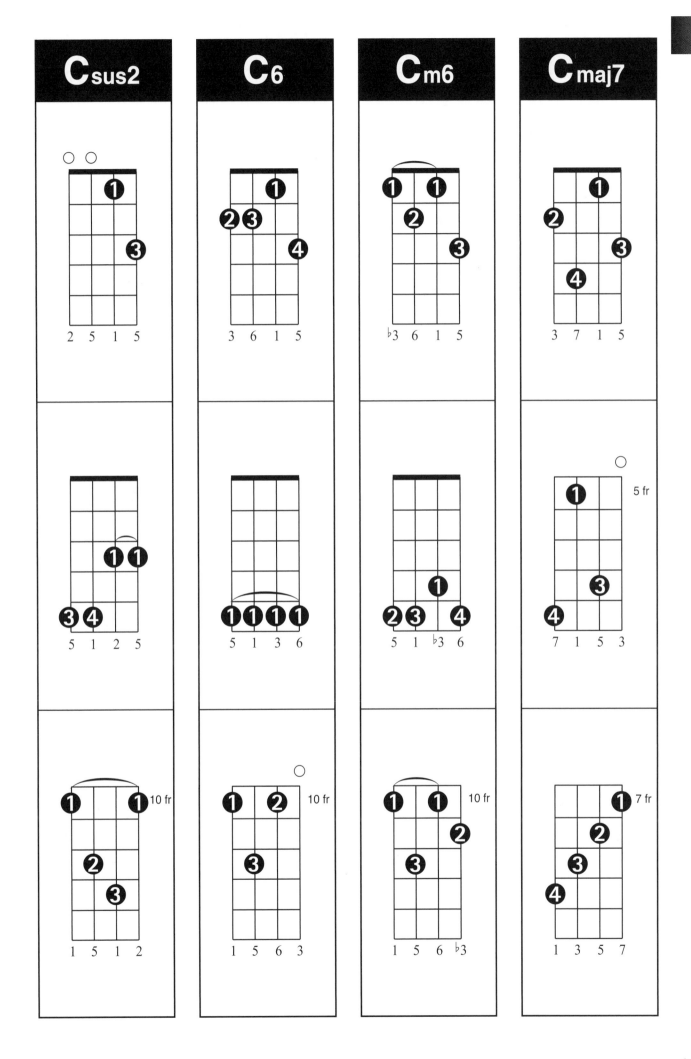

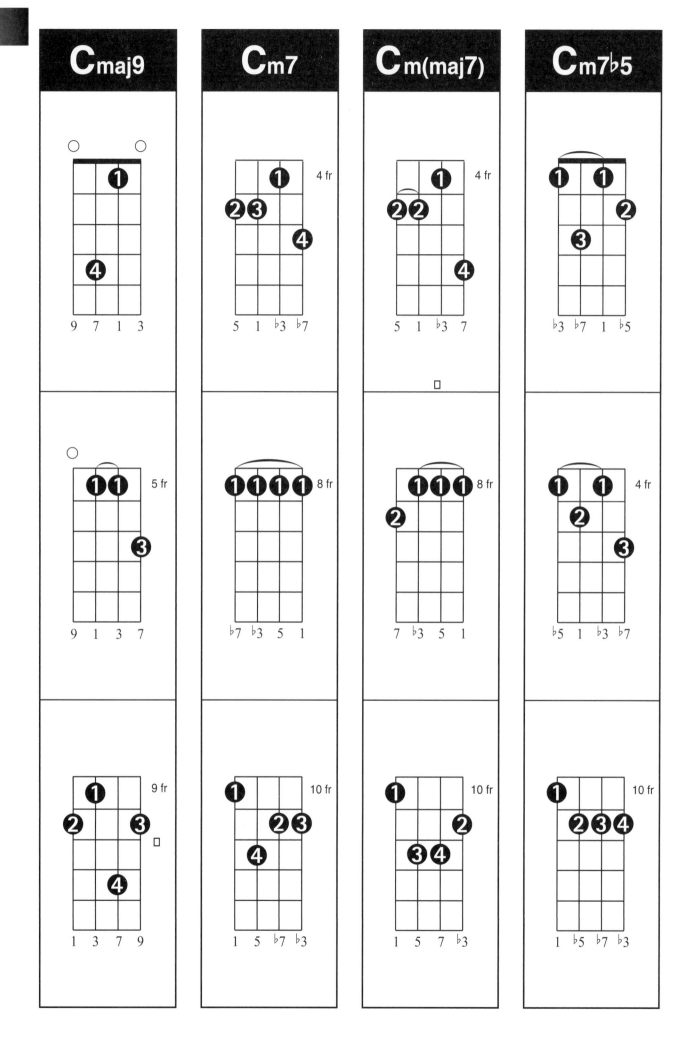

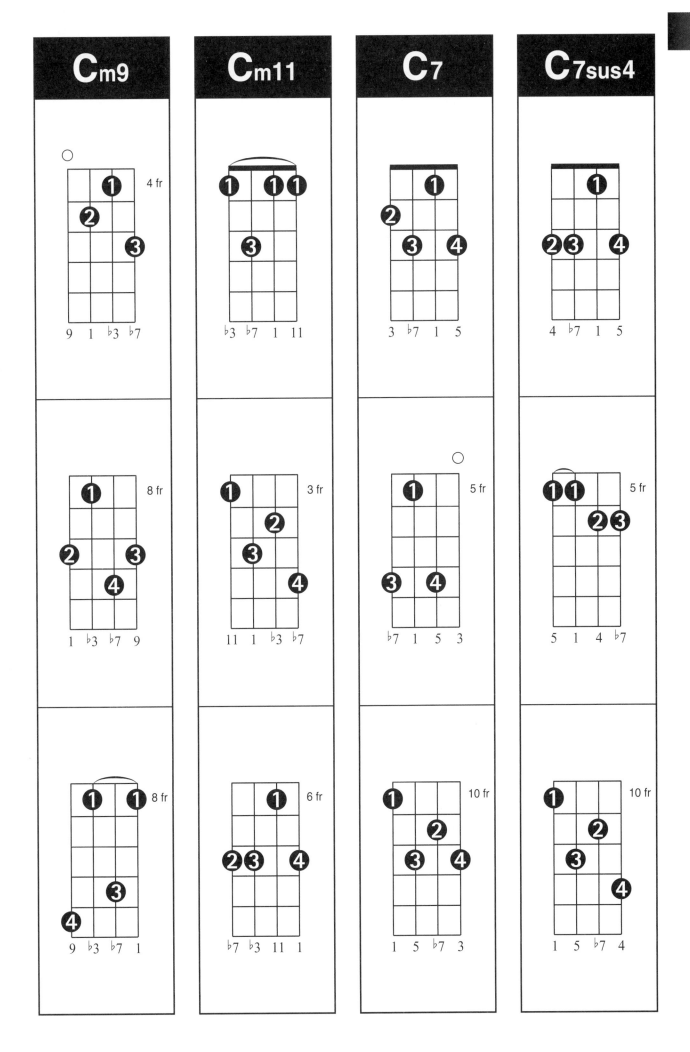

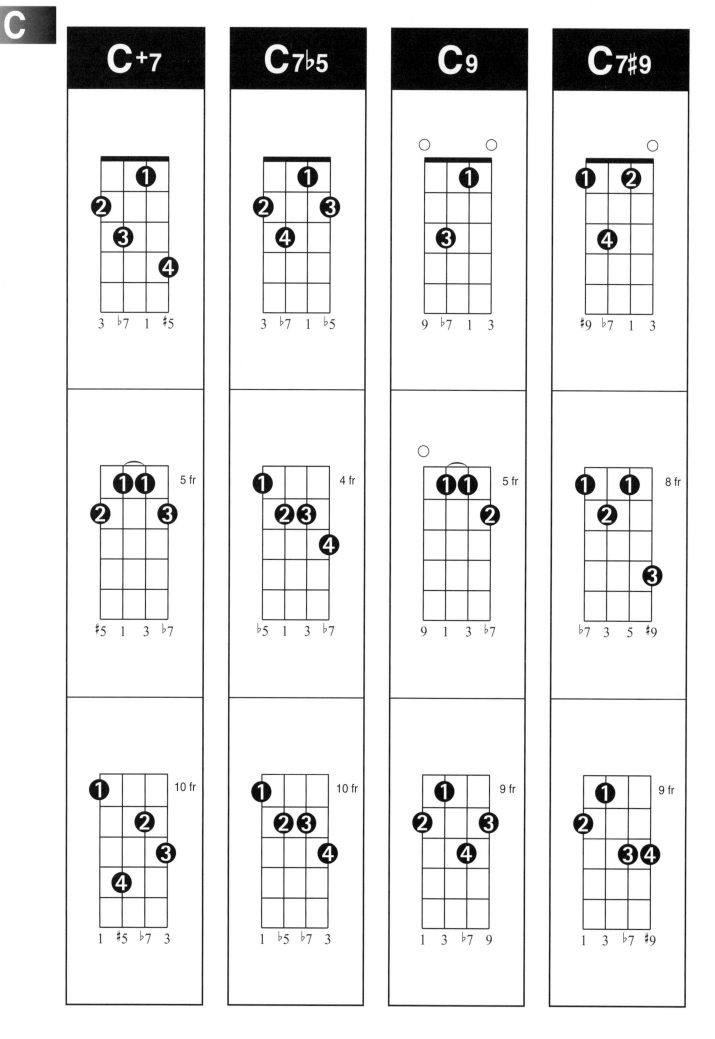

C

C+7 C7♭5 C9 C7#9

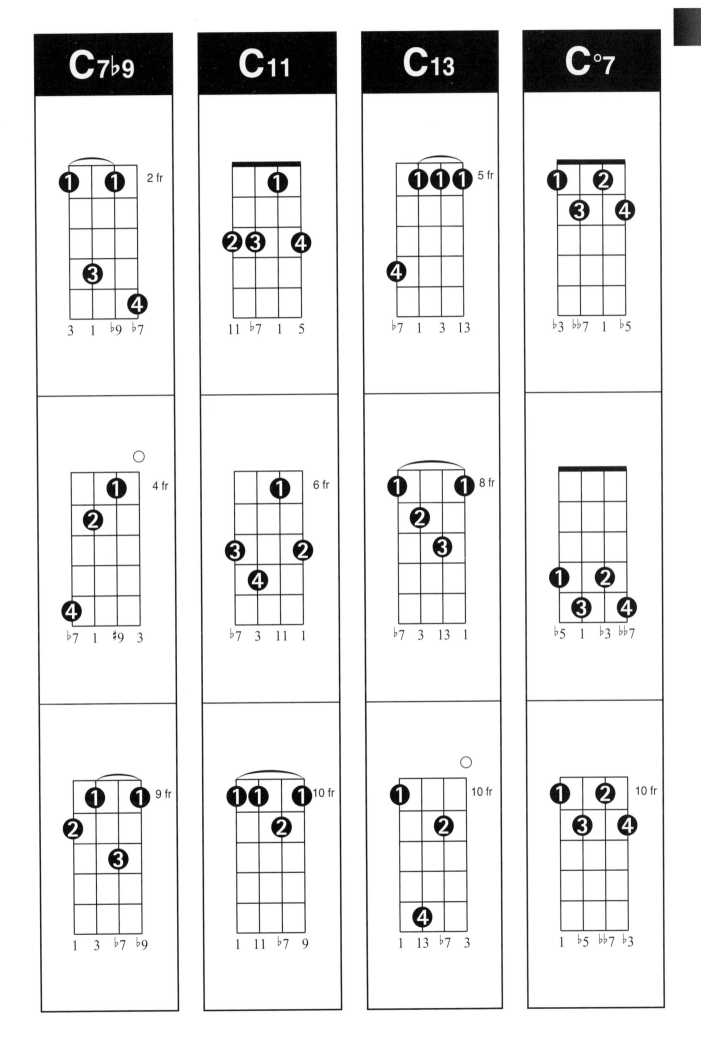

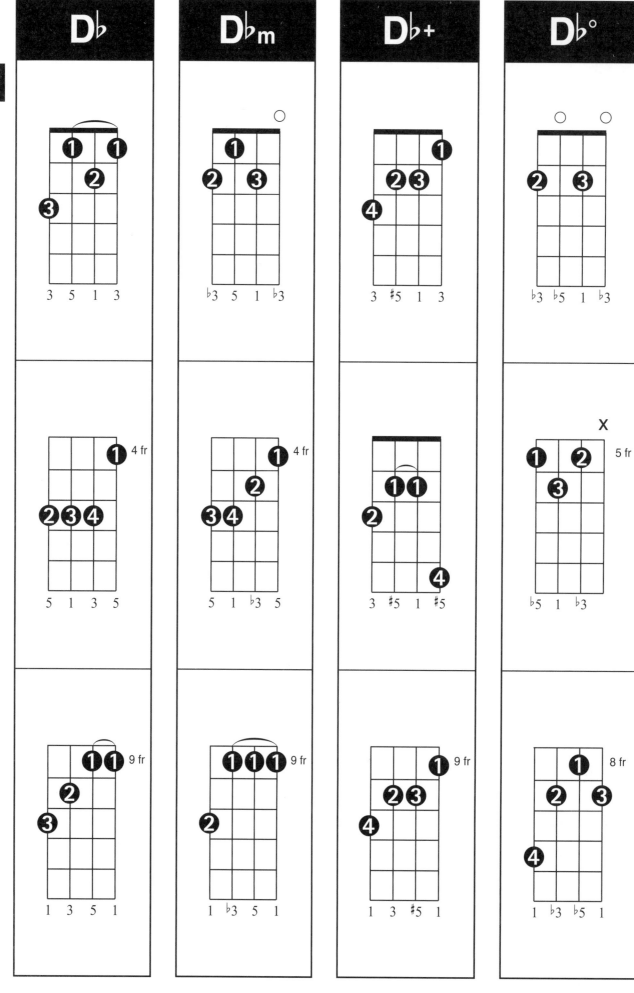

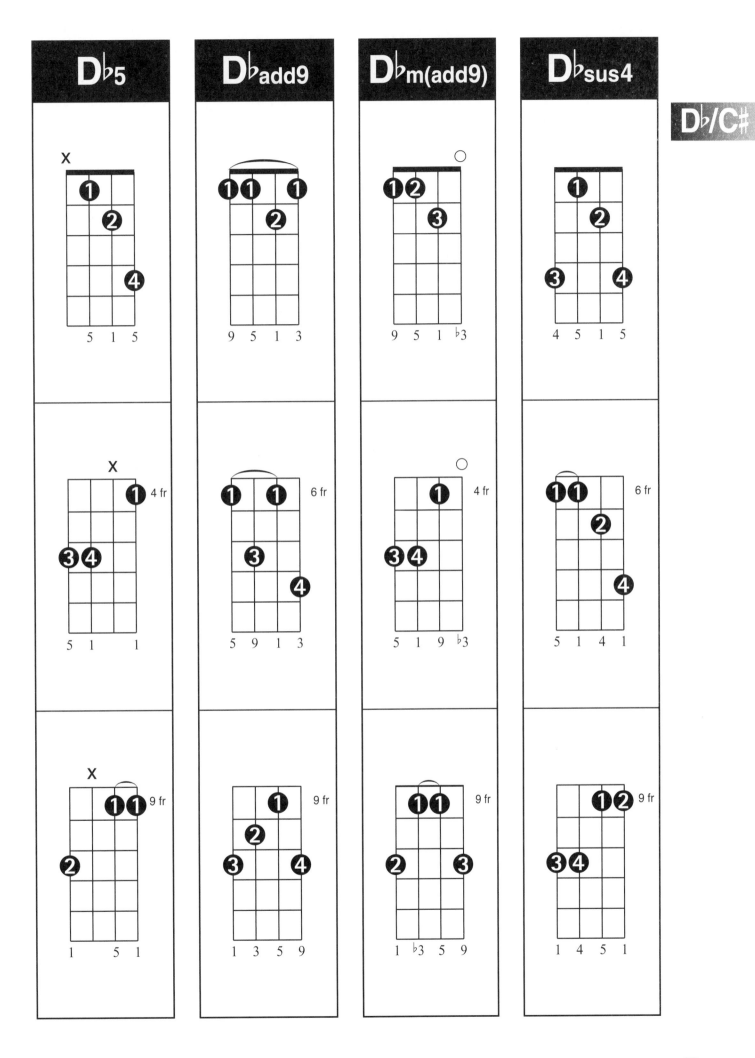

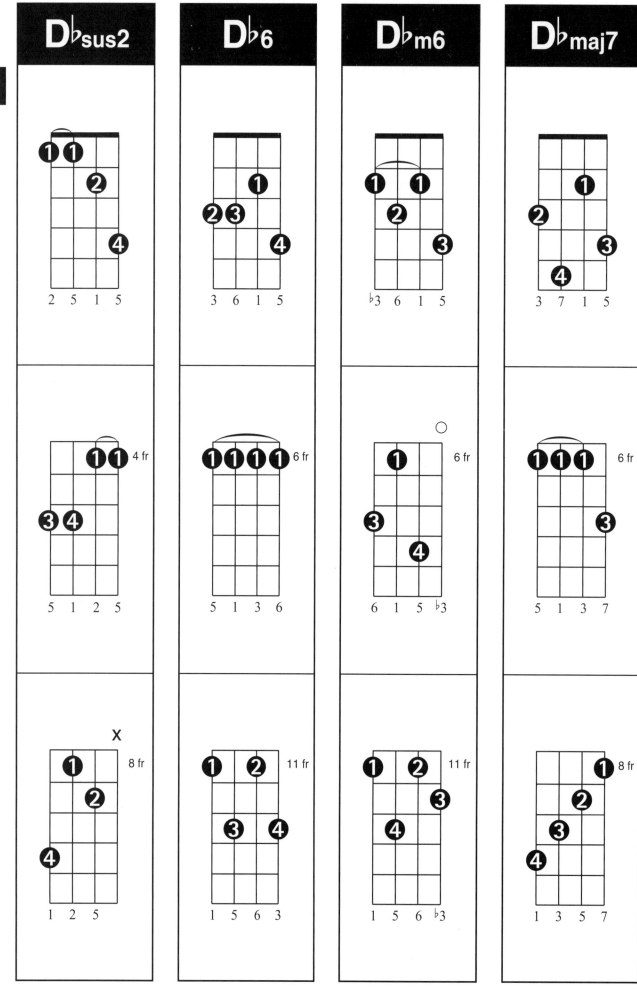

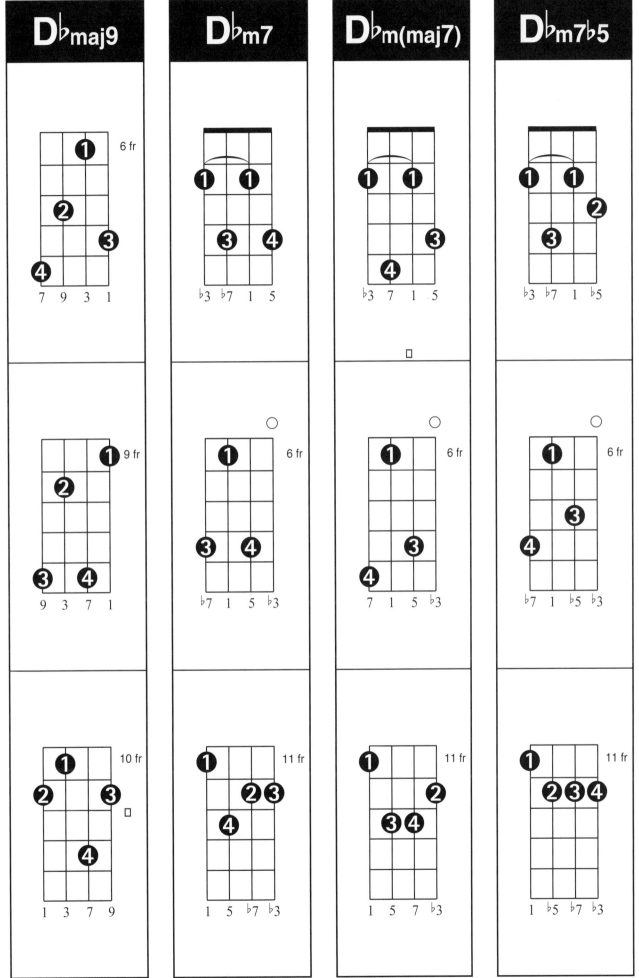

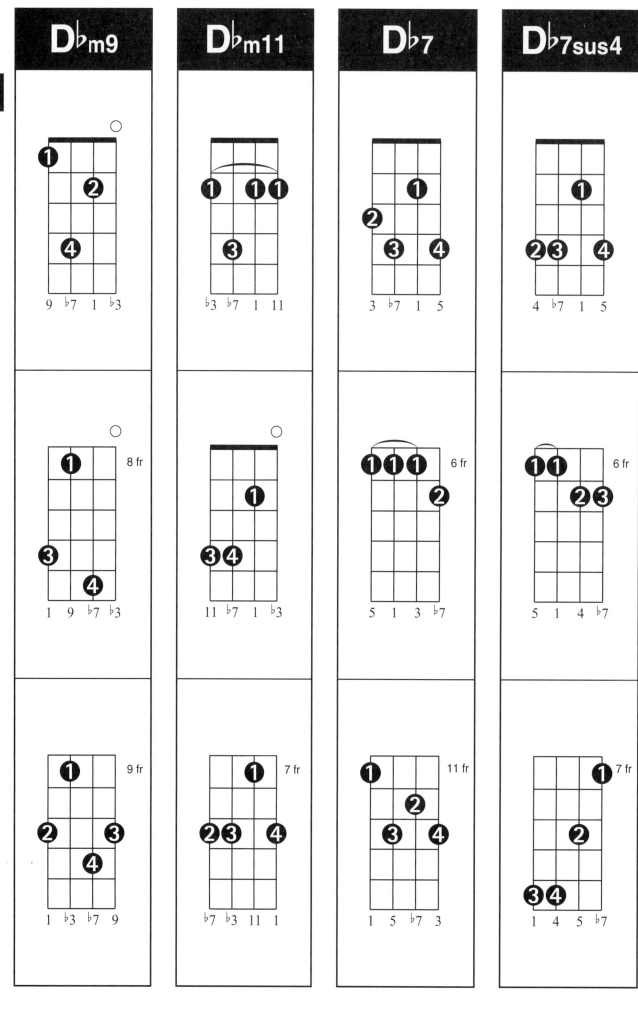

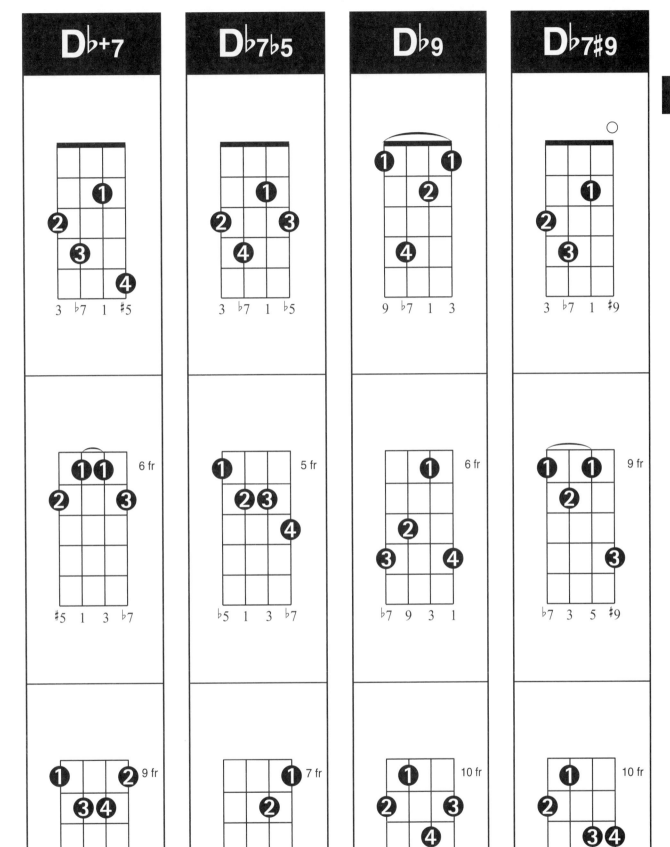

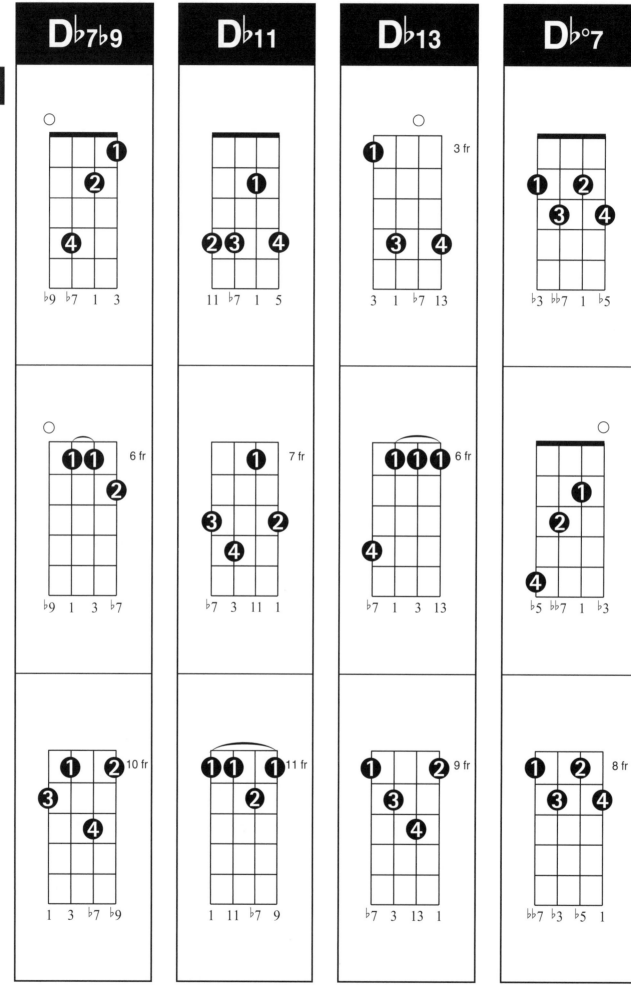

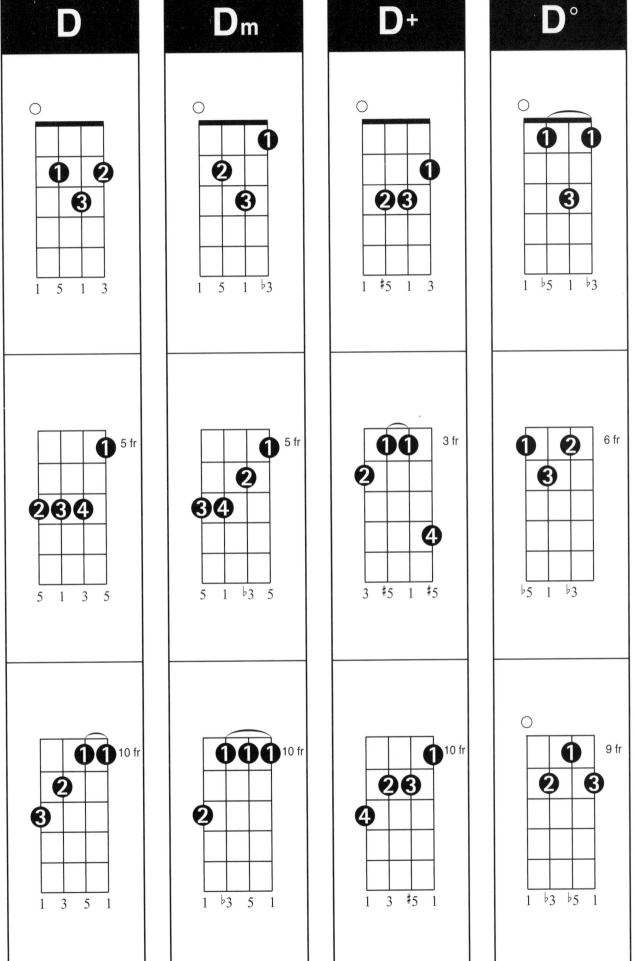

D

D5   Dadd9   Dm(add9)   Dsus4

D5

○   X

①
③

1   5   1

X

① 5 fr

③④

5   1   5

○

① 7 fr

③④

1   1   5   1

Dadd9

○

①
②
③

3   5   1   9

○

① 5 fr
②
④

1   9   3   5

① 10 fr
②
③   ④

1   3   5   9

Dm(add9)

○

①
②③

♭3   5   1   9

○

① 5 fr
②
④

1   9   ♭3   5

①② 10 fr
③   ④

1   ♭3   5   9

Dsus4

○

①
③④

1   5   1   4

① 5 fr
②③
④

5   1   4   5

①① 7 fr
②
④

5   1   4   1

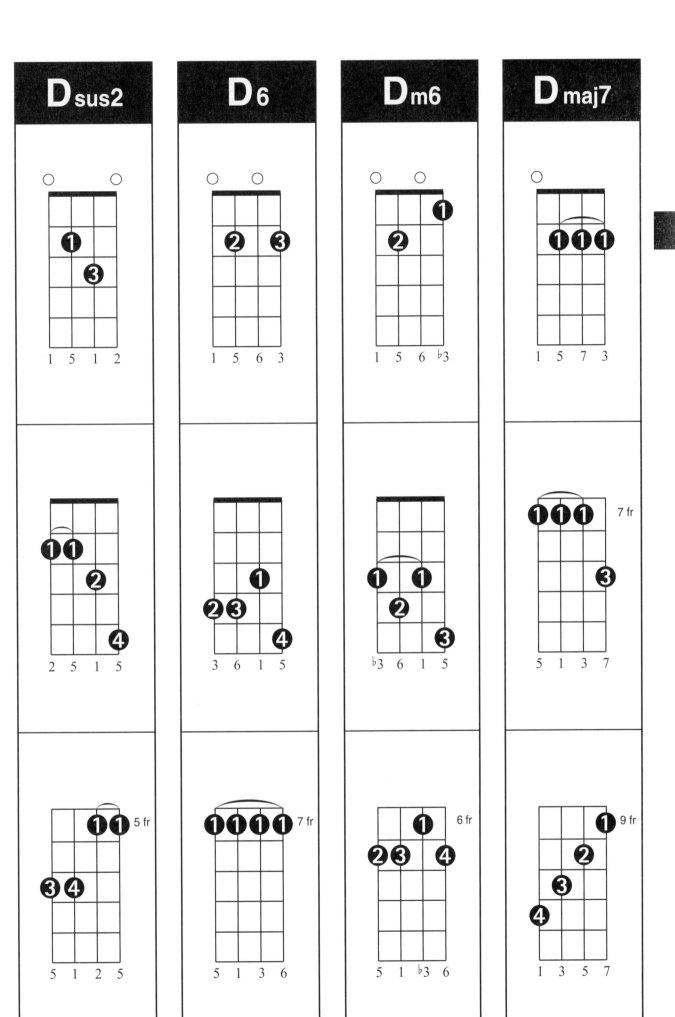

D maj9

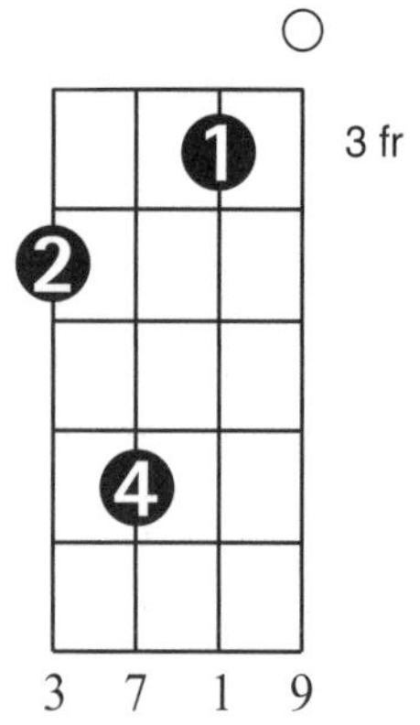

3 fr

3　7　1　9

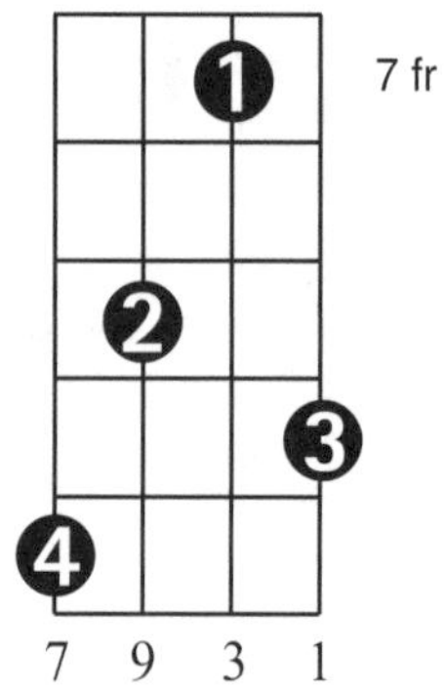

7 fr

7　9　3　1

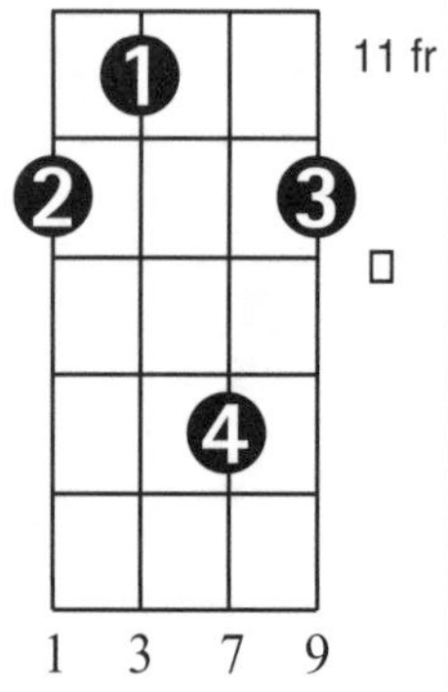

11 fr

1　3　7　9

D m7

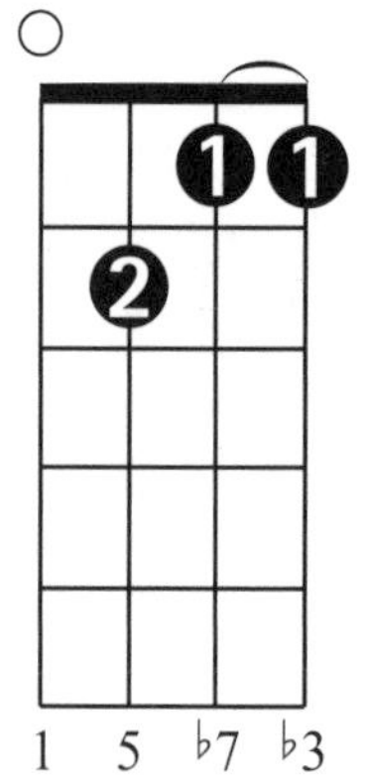

1　5　♭7　♭3

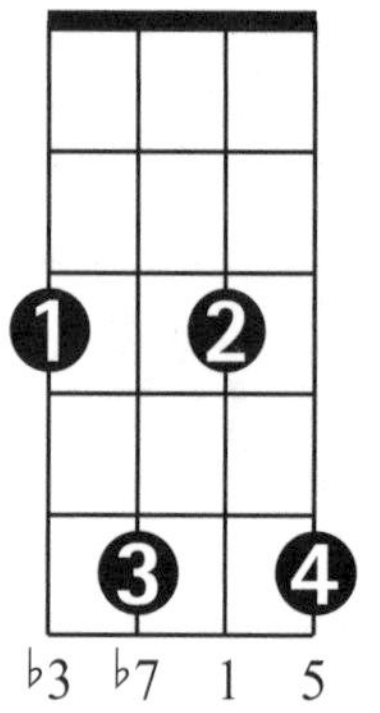

♭3　♭7　1　5

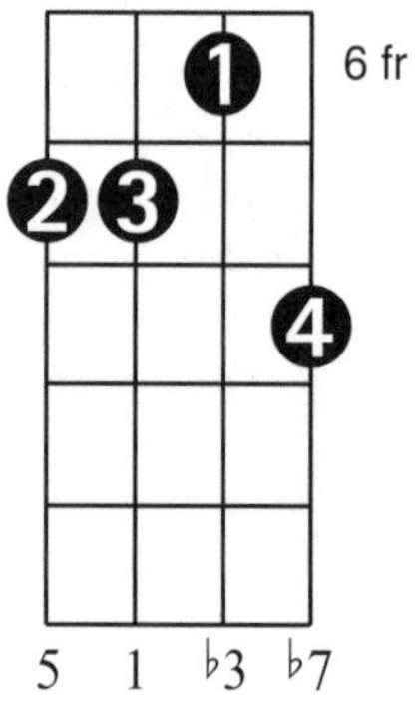

6 fr

5　1　♭3　♭7

D m(maj7)

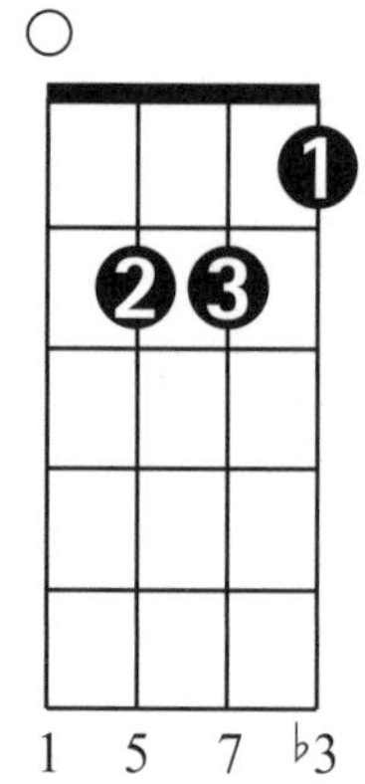

1　5　7　♭3

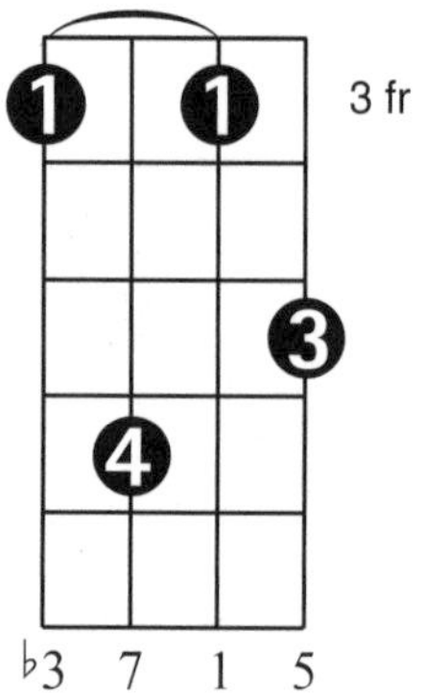

3 fr

♭3　7　1　5

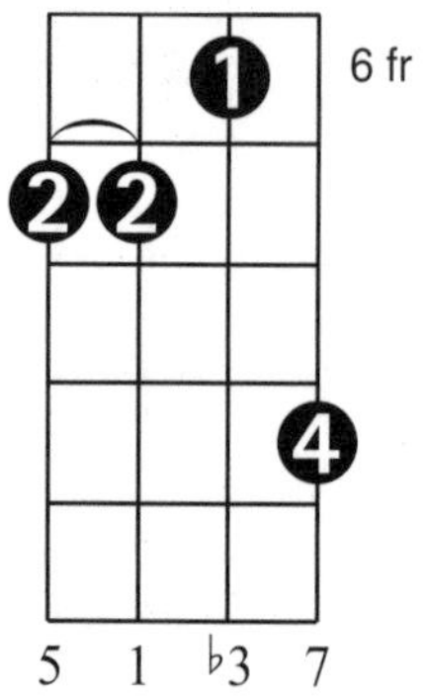

6 fr

5　1　♭3　7

D m7♭5

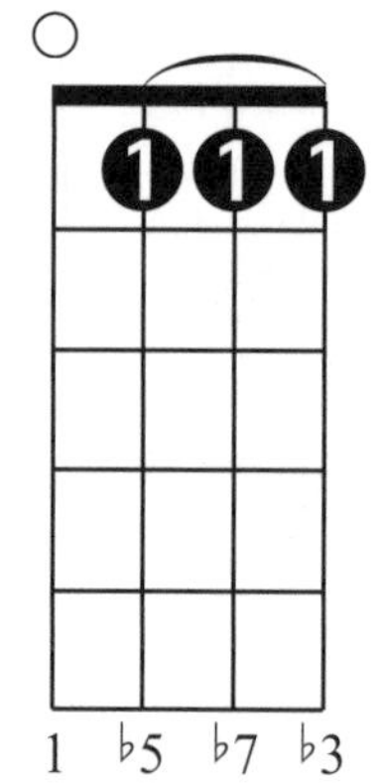

1　♭5　♭7　♭3

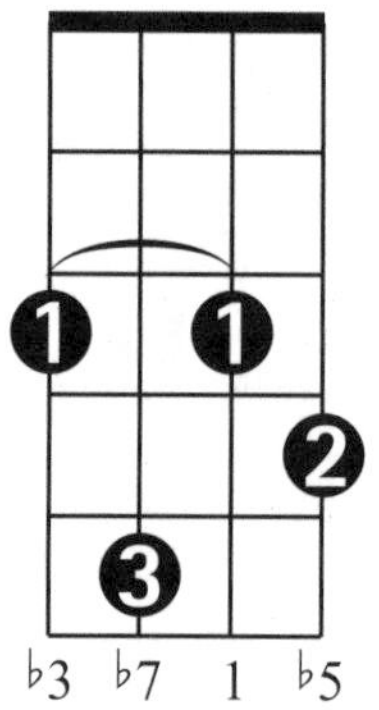

♭3　♭7　1　♭5

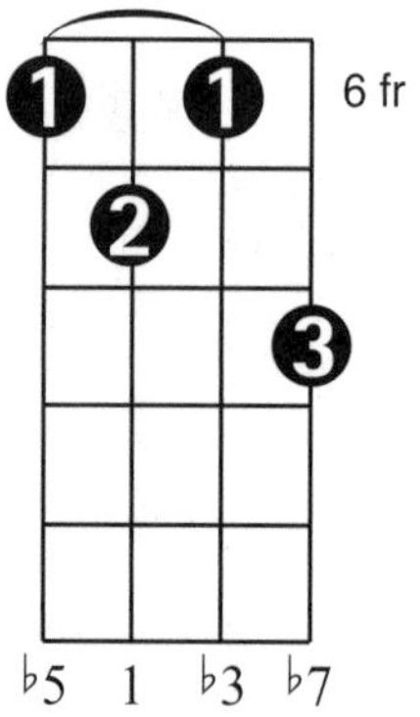

6 fr

♭5　1　♭3　♭7

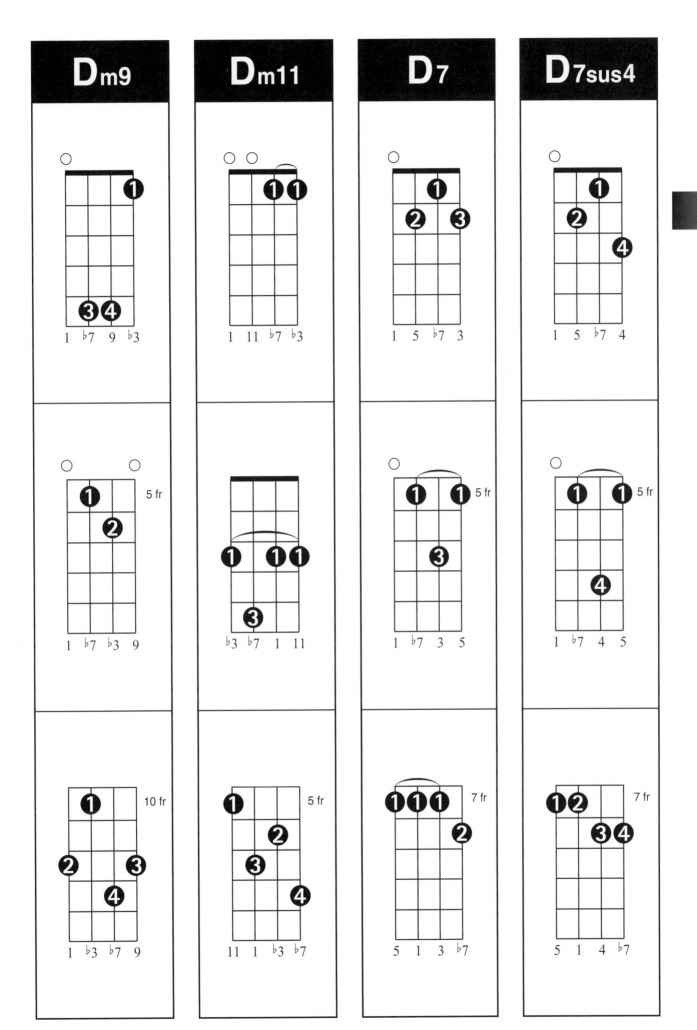

D+7

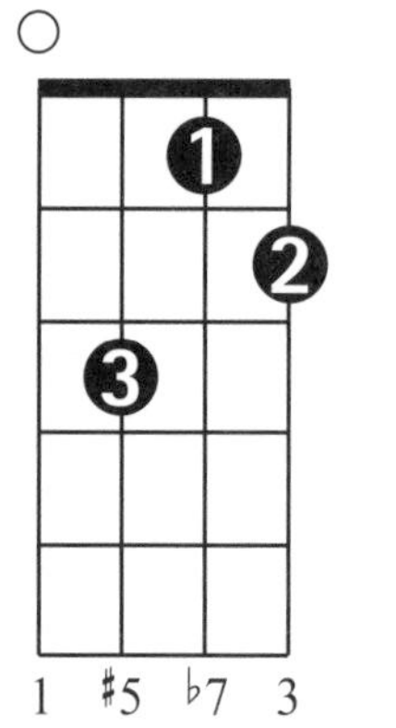

1 #5 ♭7 3

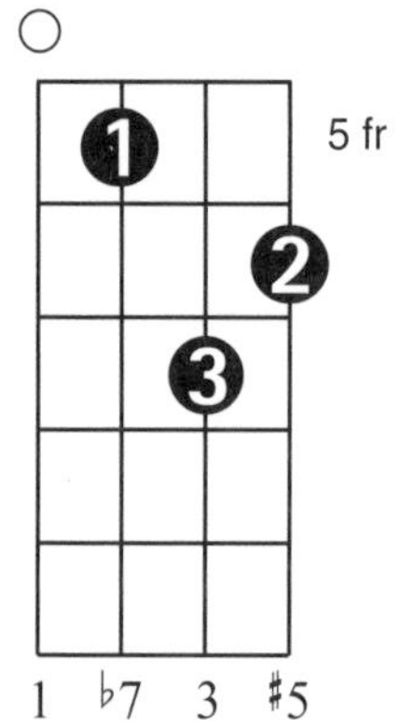

5 fr

1 ♭7 3 #5

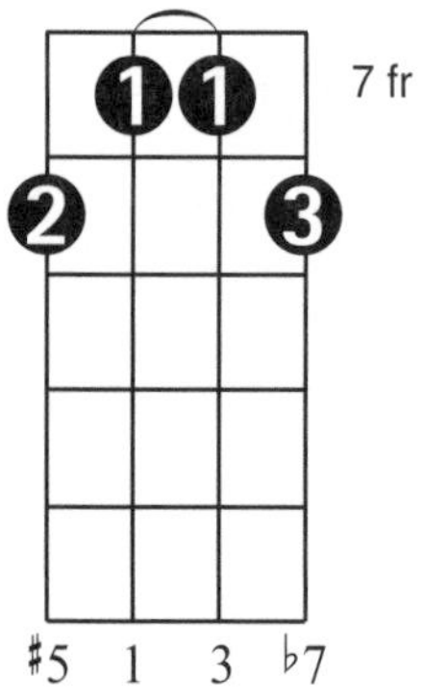

7 fr

#5 1 3 ♭7

D7♭5

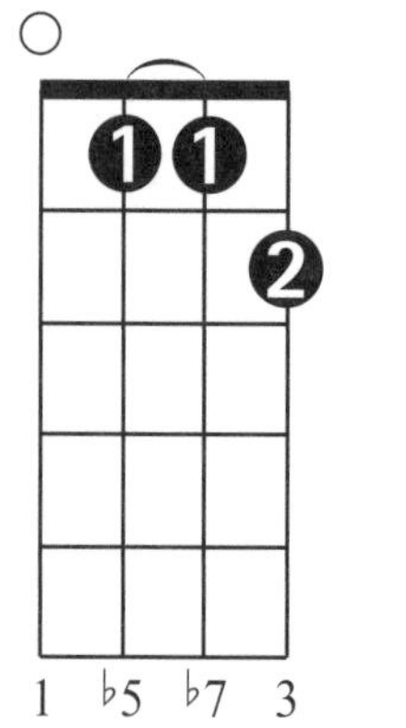

1 ♭5 ♭7 3

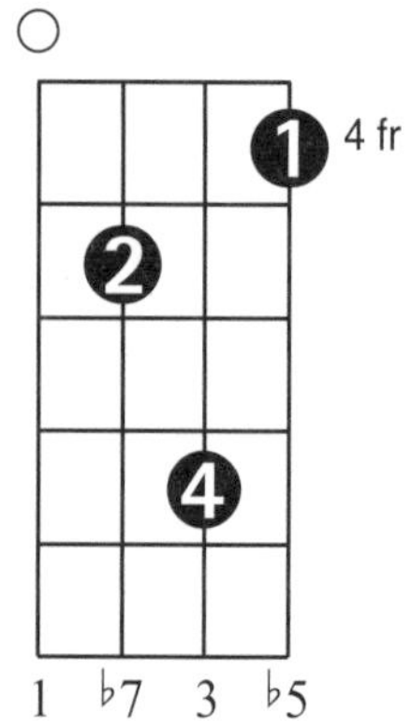

4 fr

1 ♭7 3 ♭5

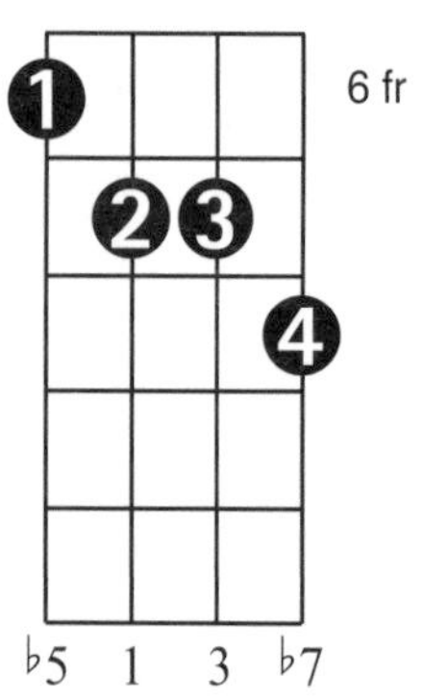

6 fr

♭5 1 3 ♭7

D9

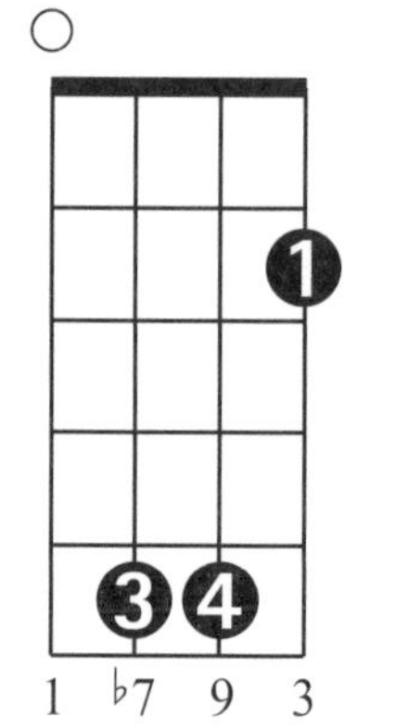

1 ♭7 9 3

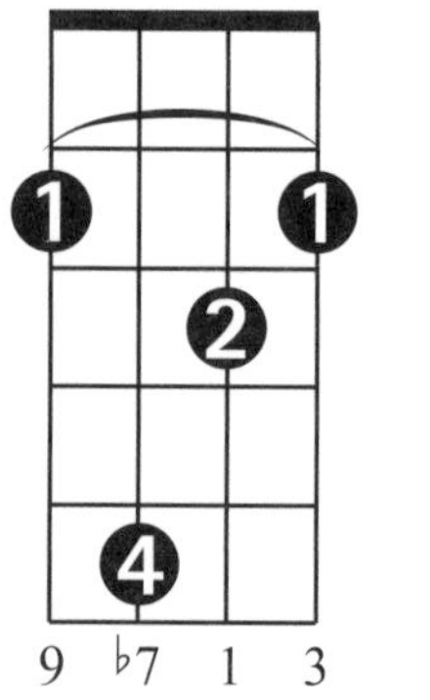

9 ♭7 1 3

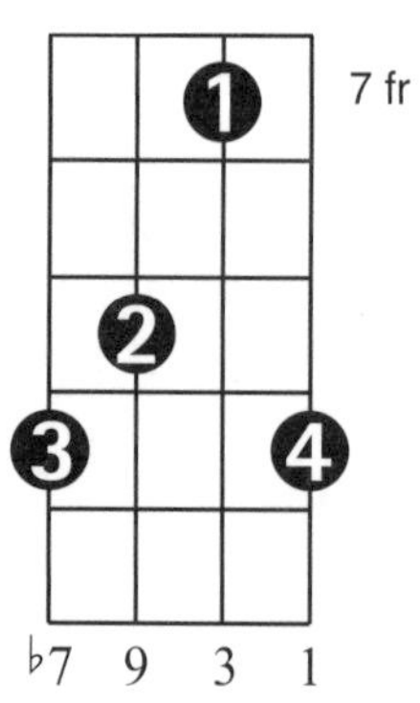

7 fr

♭7 9 3 1

D7#9

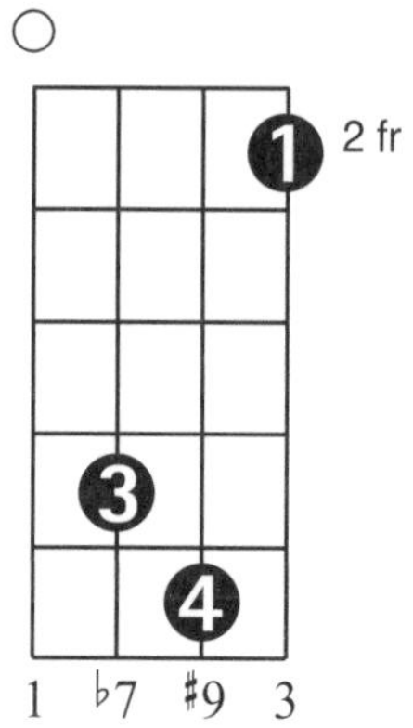

2 fr

1 ♭7 #9 3

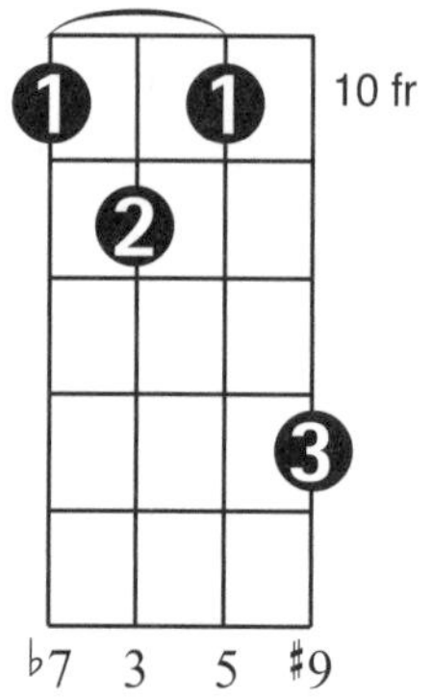

10 fr

♭7 3 5 #9

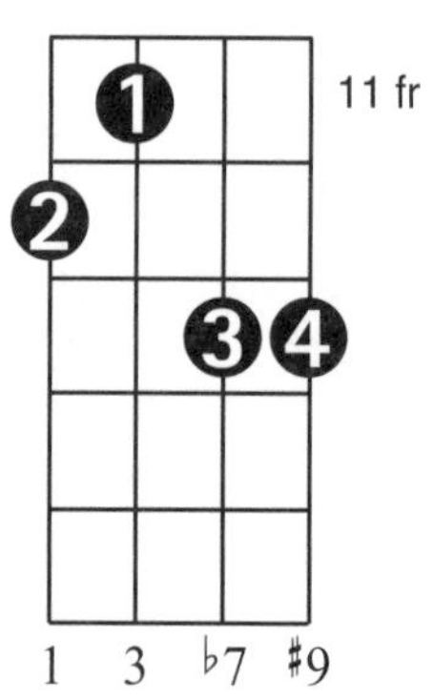

11 fr

1 3 ♭7 #9

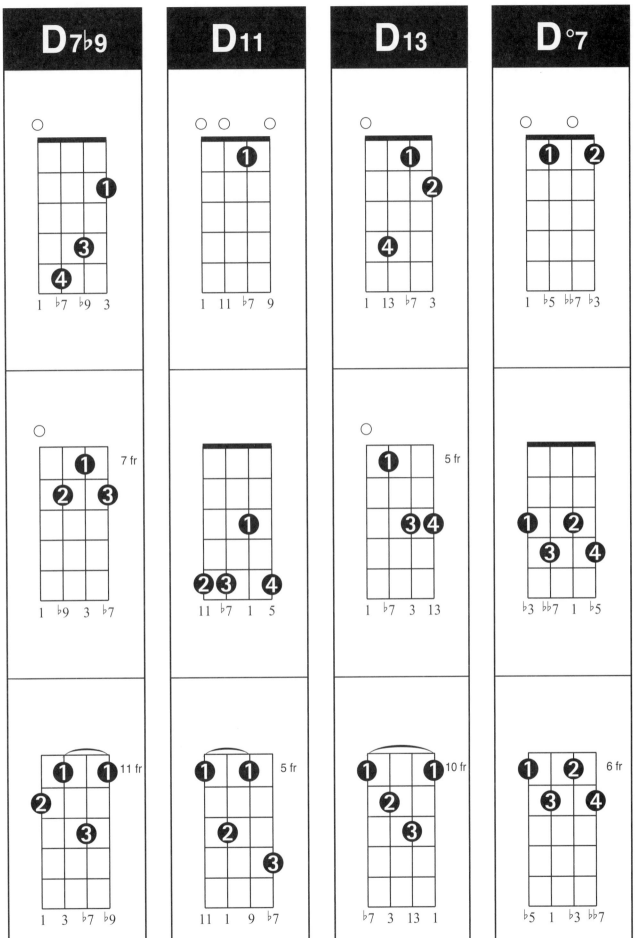

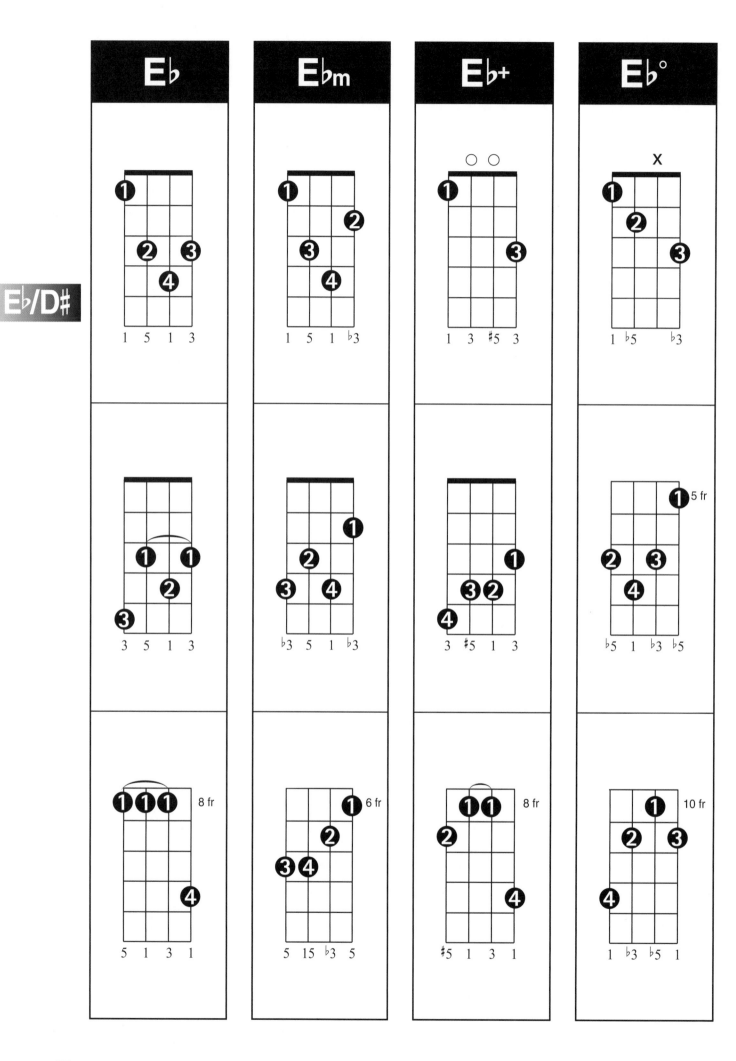

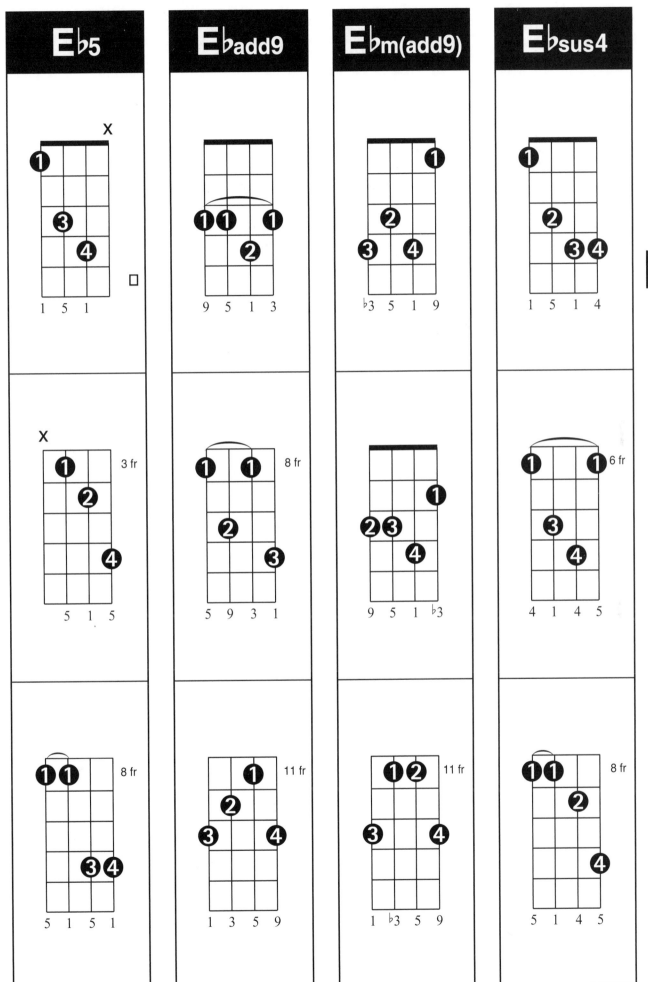

Eb5

Ebadd9

Ebm(add9)

Ebsus4

Eb/D#

31

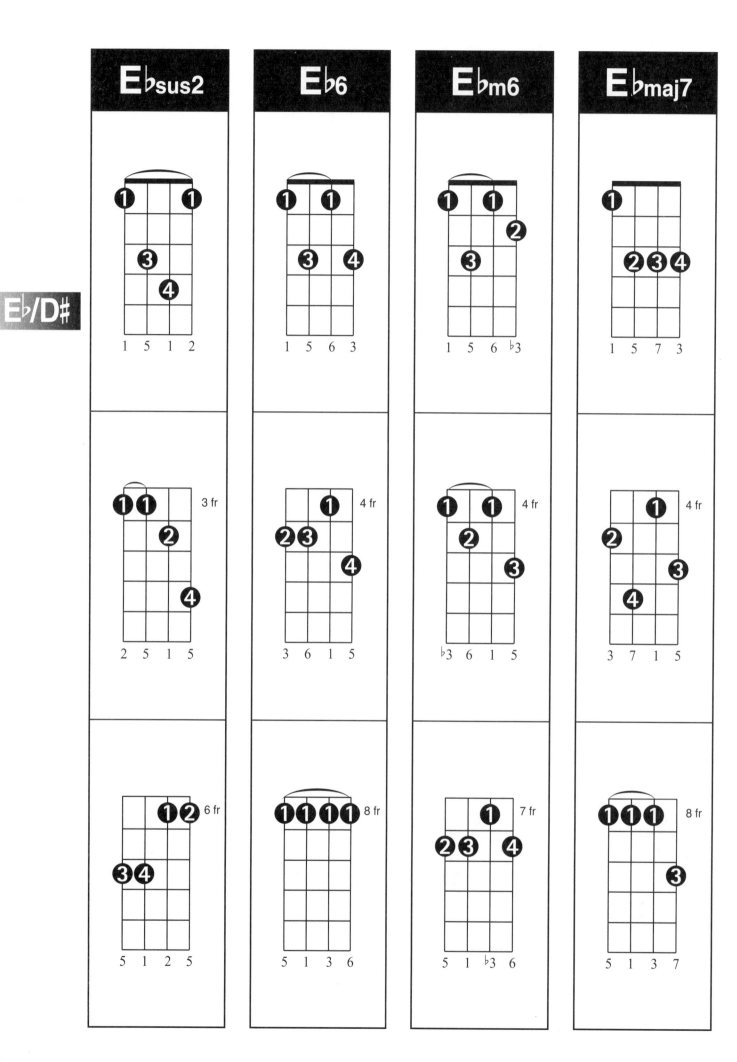

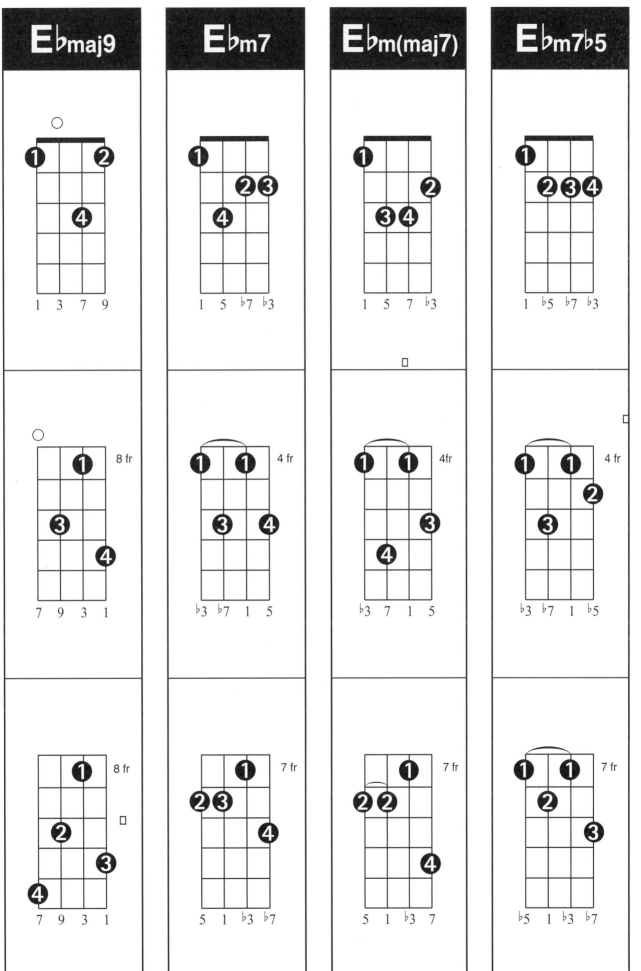

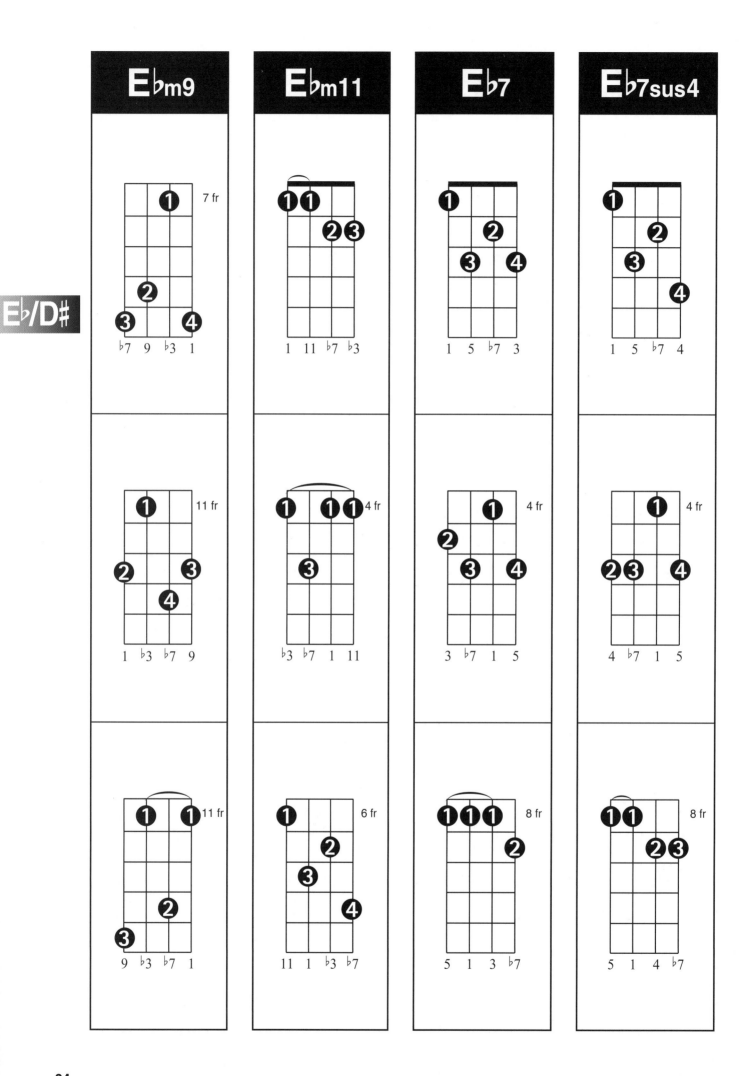

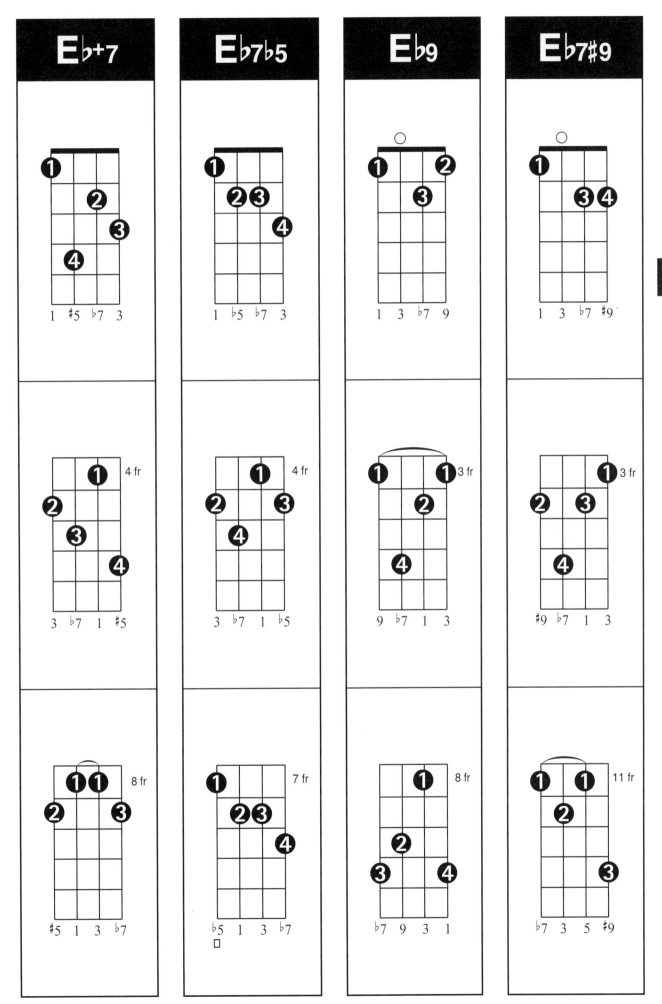

E♭7♭9　E♭11　E♭13　E♭°7

E♭/D#

E♭7♭9

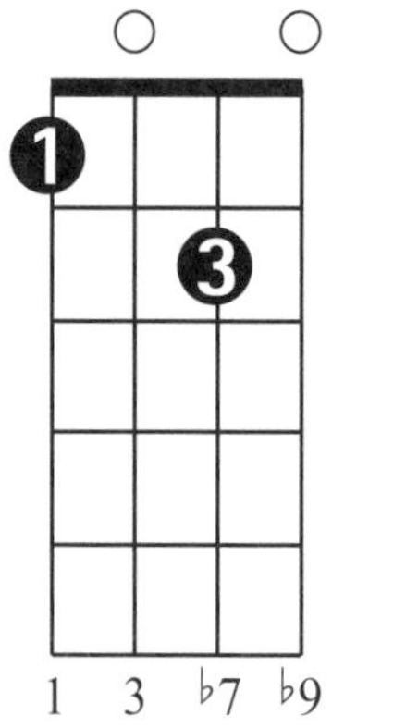

1 3 ♭7 ♭9

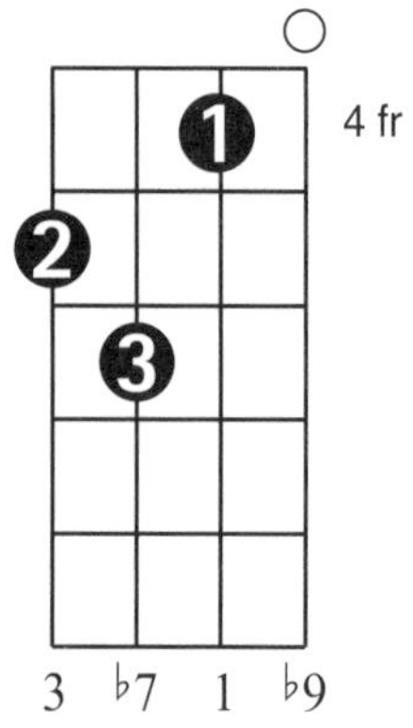

4 fr
3 ♭7 1 ♭9

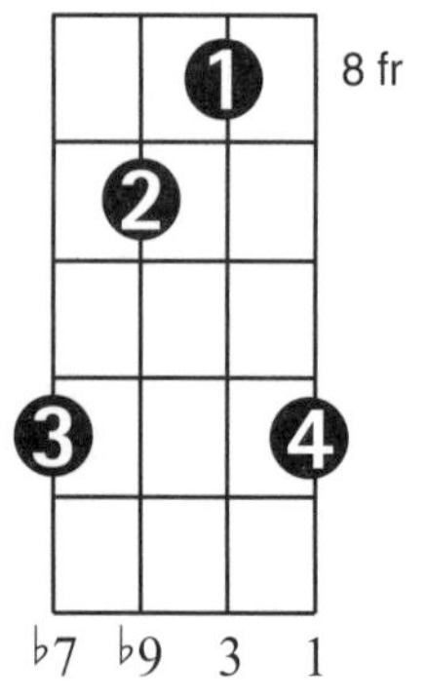

8 fr
♭7 ♭9 3 1

E♭11

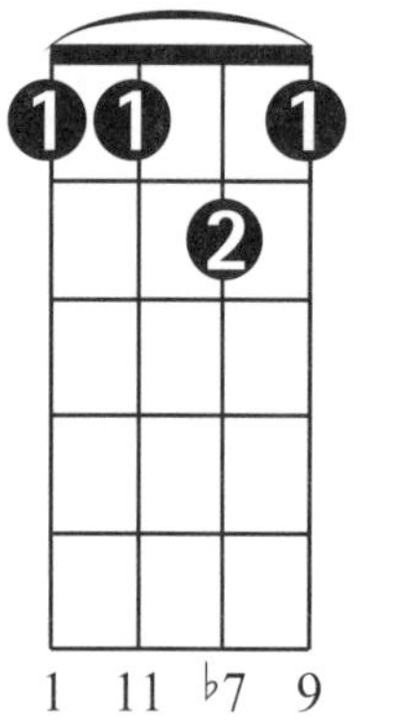

1 11 ♭7 9

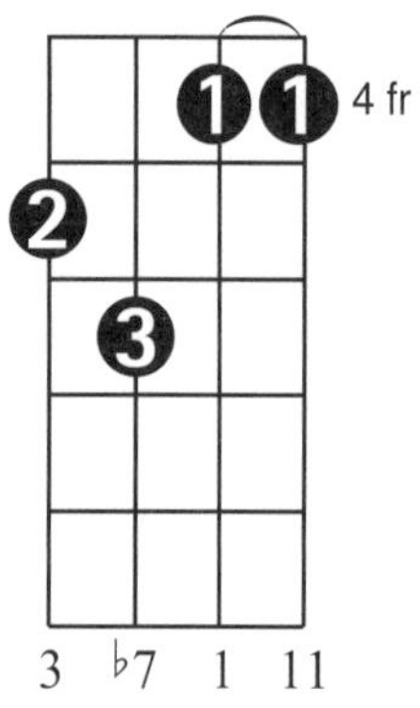

4 fr
3 ♭7 1 11

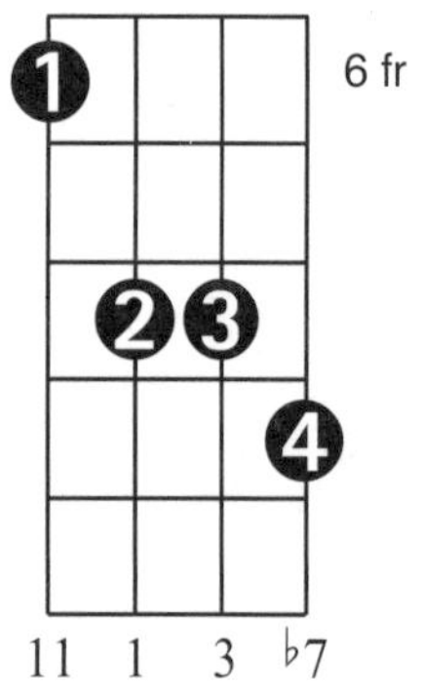

6 fr
11 1 3 ♭7

E♭13

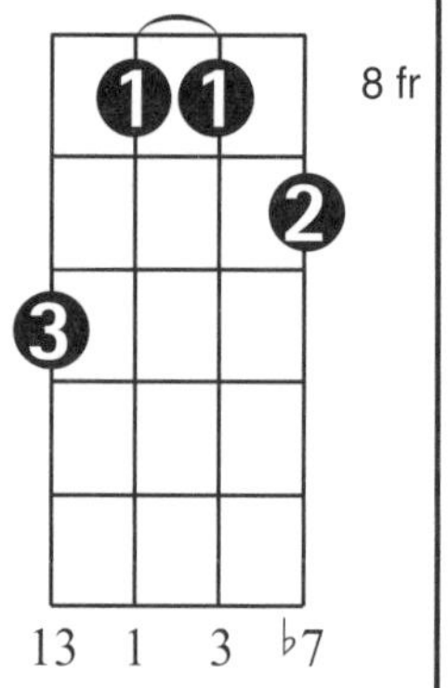

8 fr
13 1 3 ♭7

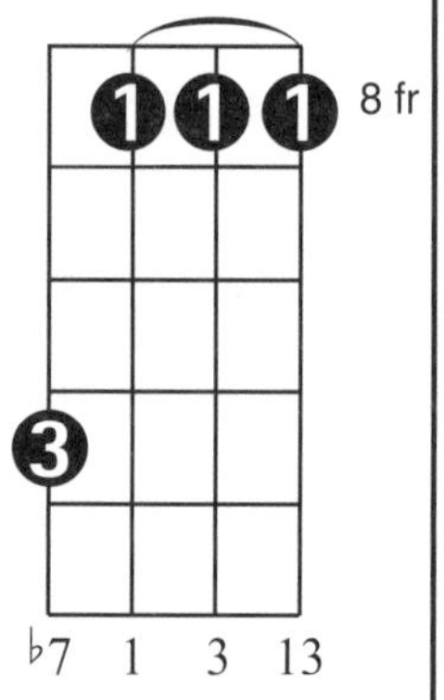

8 fr
♭7 1 3 13

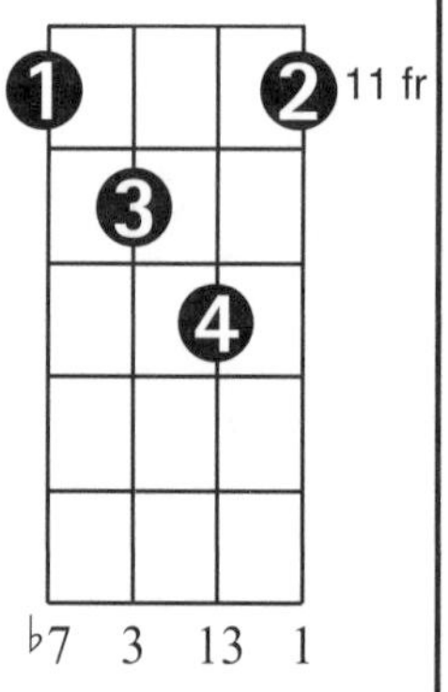

11 fr
♭7 3 13 1

E♭°7

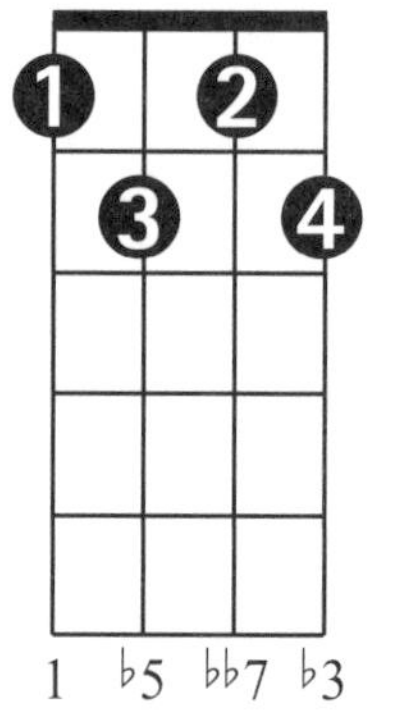

1 ♭5 ♭♭7 ♭3

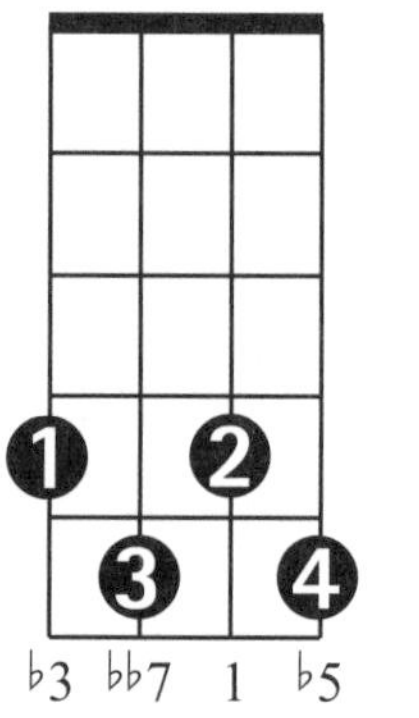

♭3 ♭♭7 1 ♭5

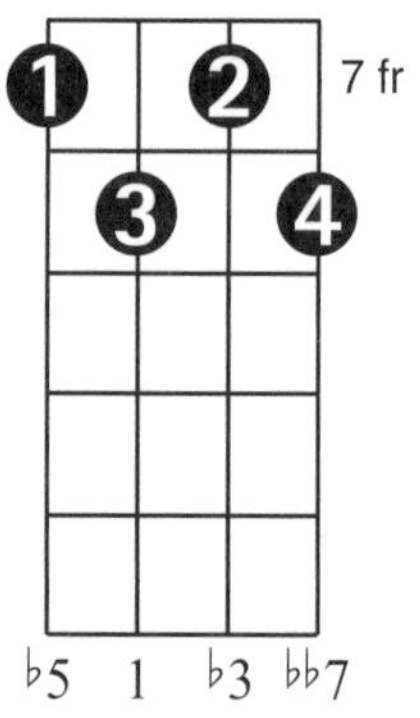

7 fr
♭5 1 ♭3 ♭♭7

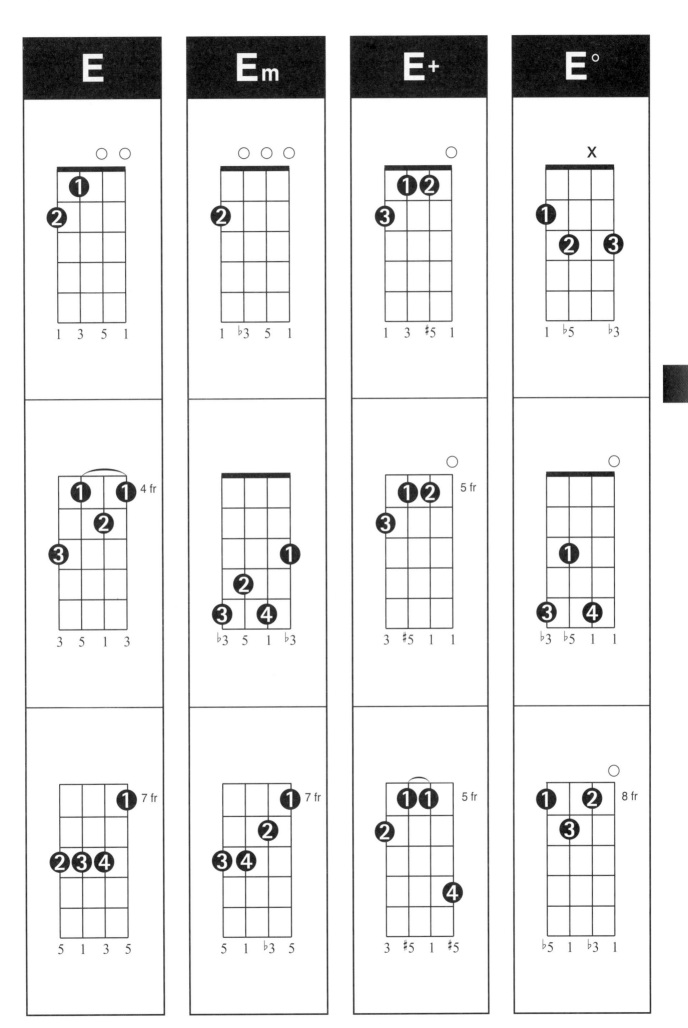

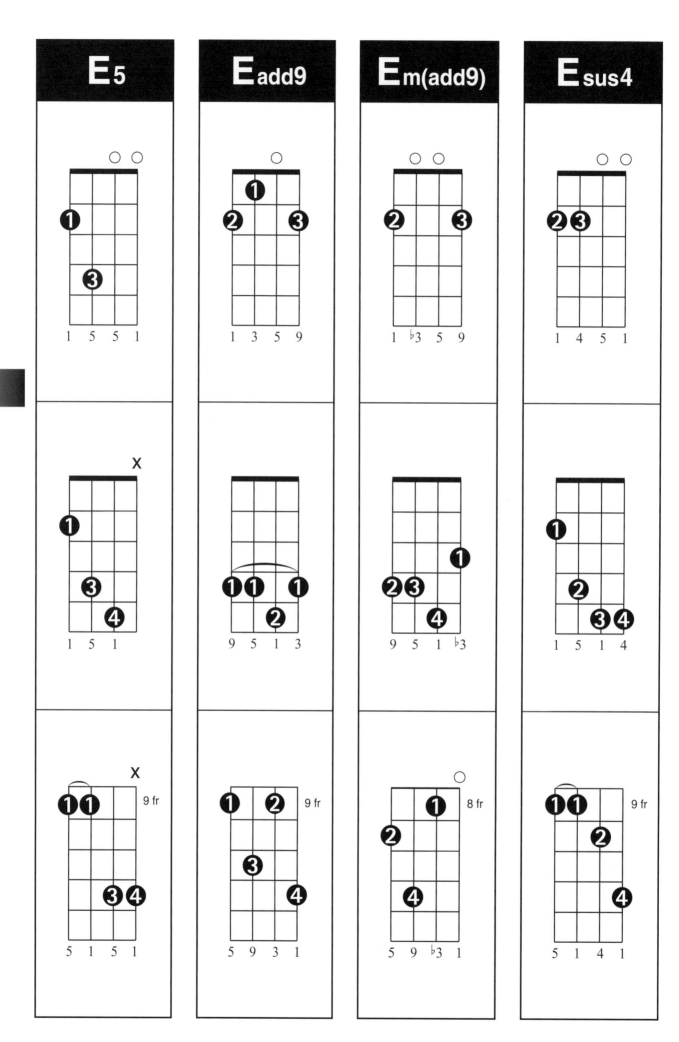

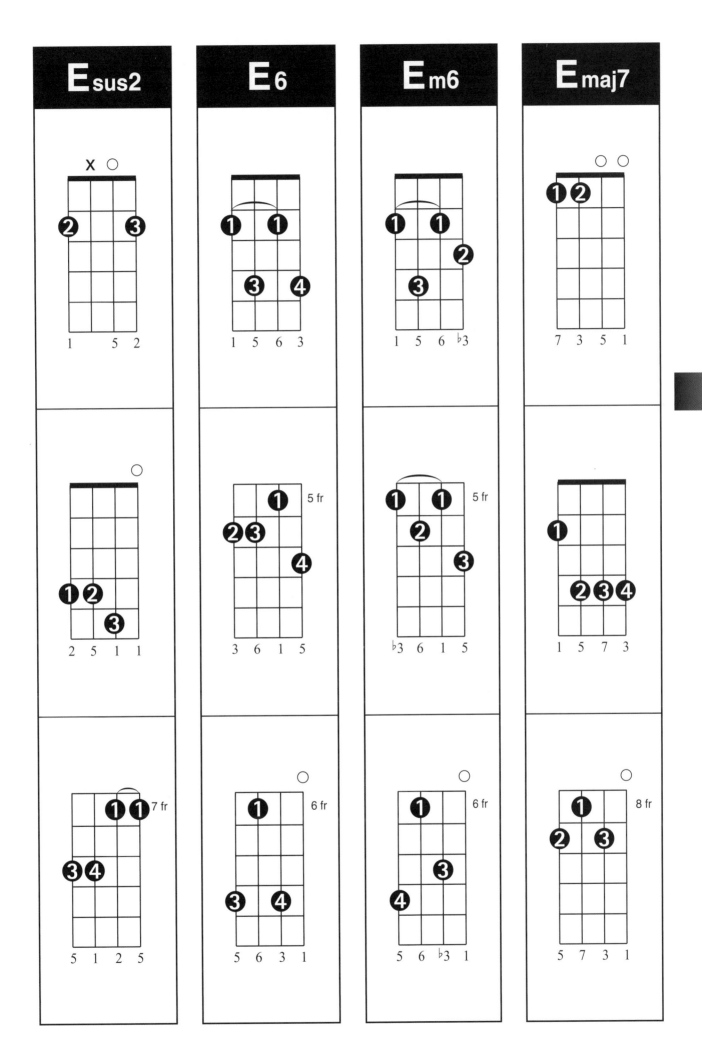

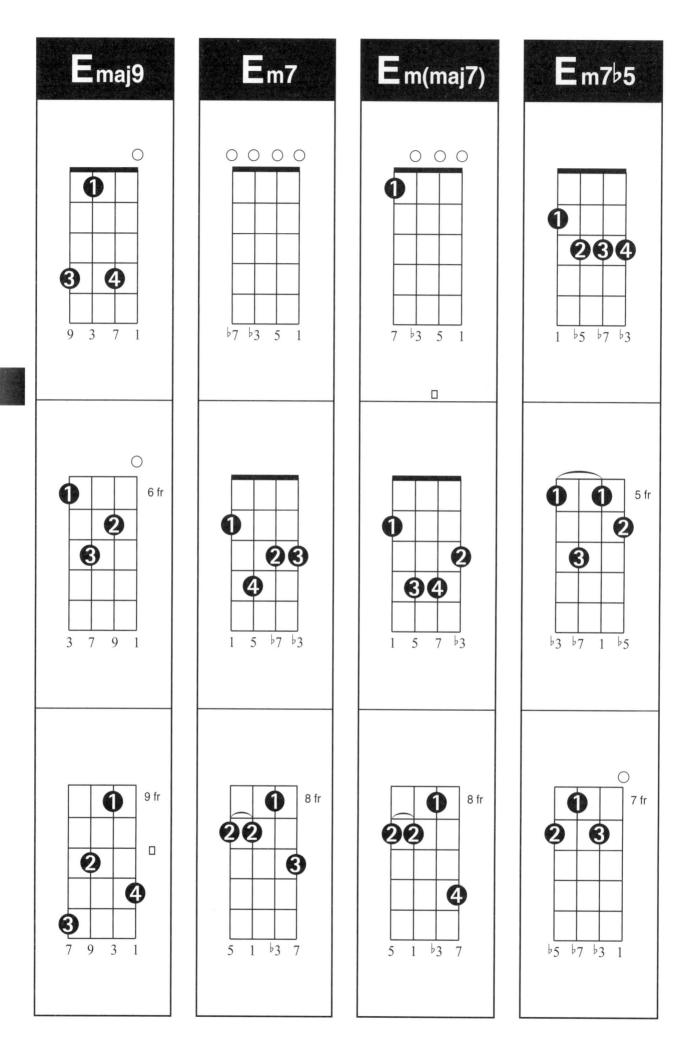

E

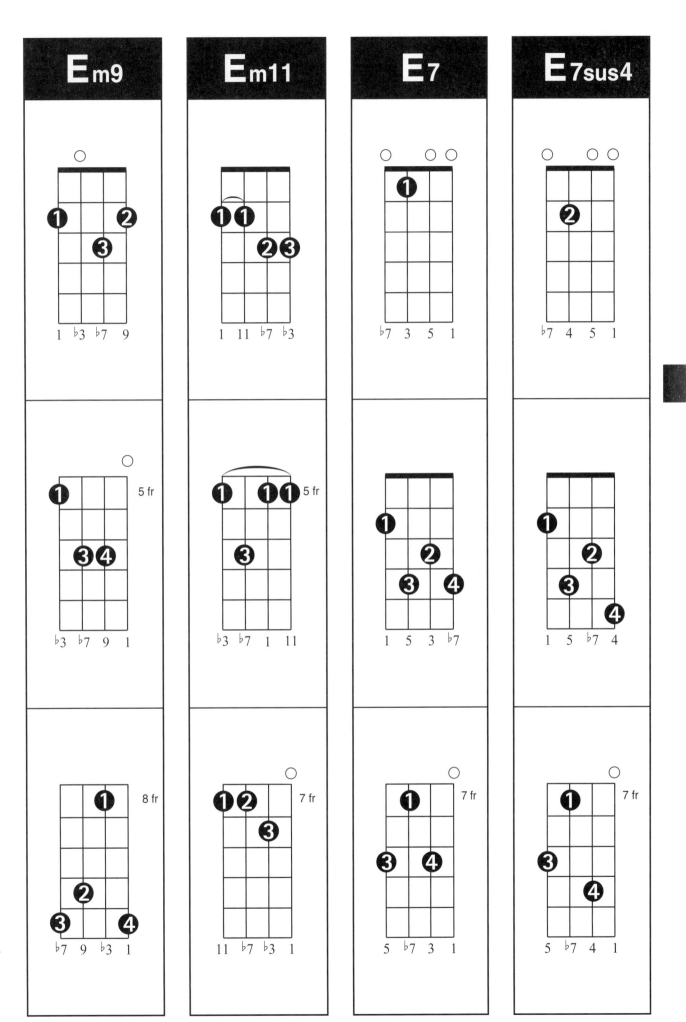

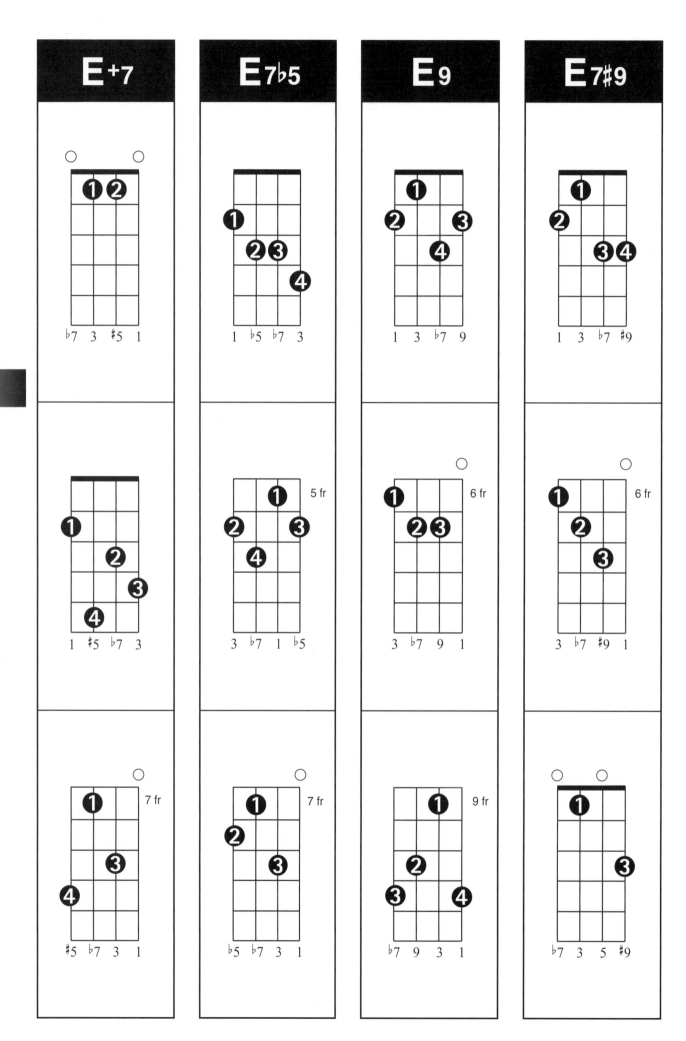

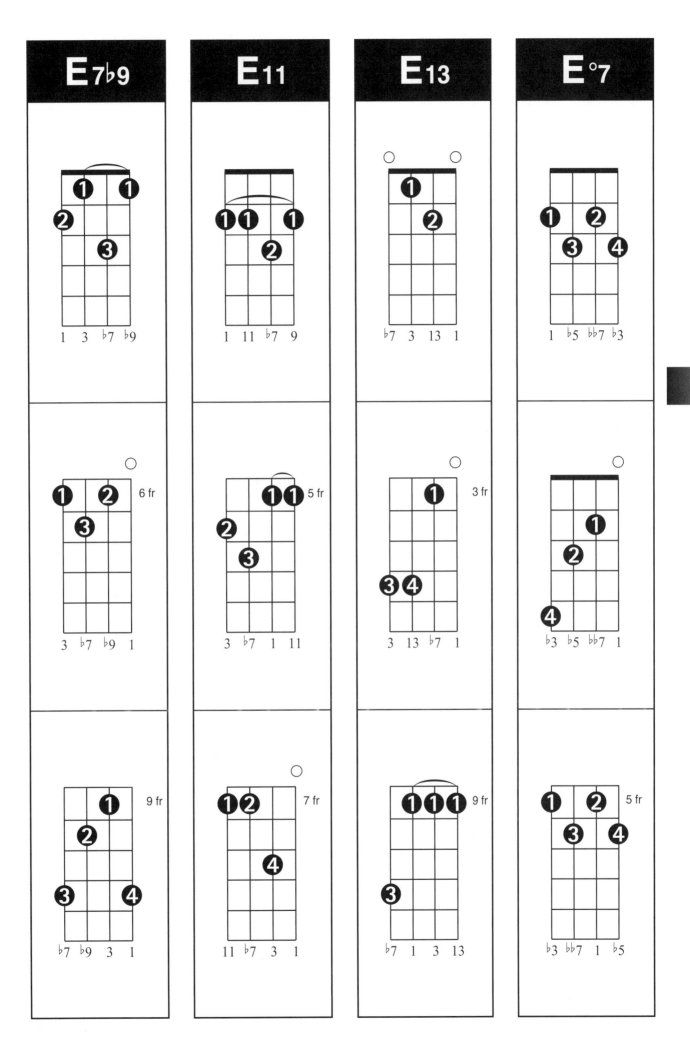

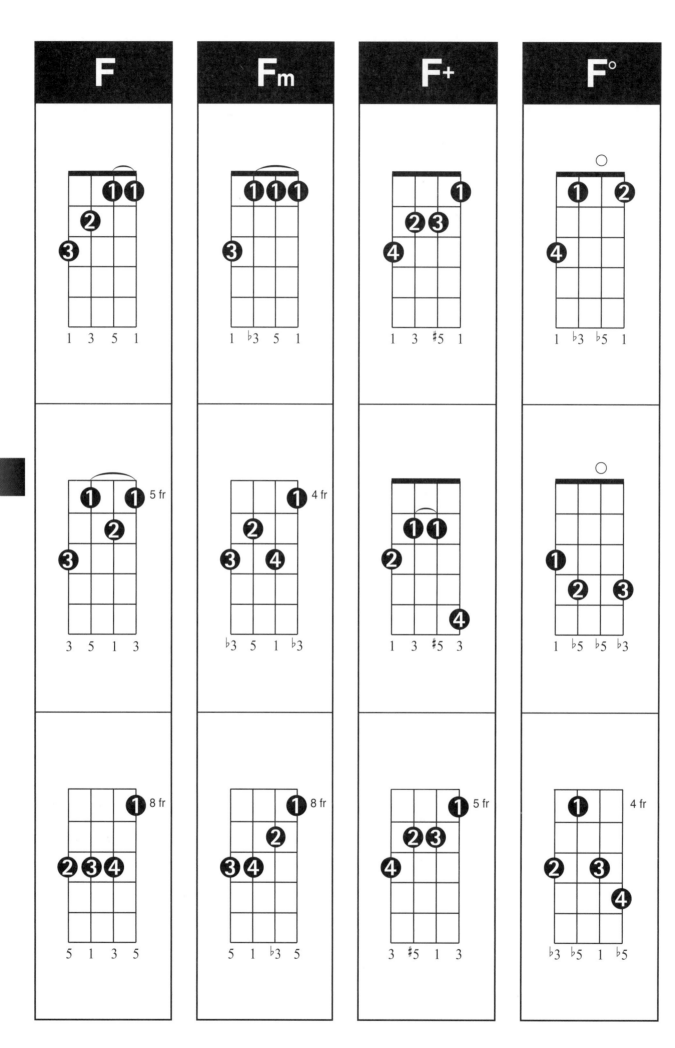

F

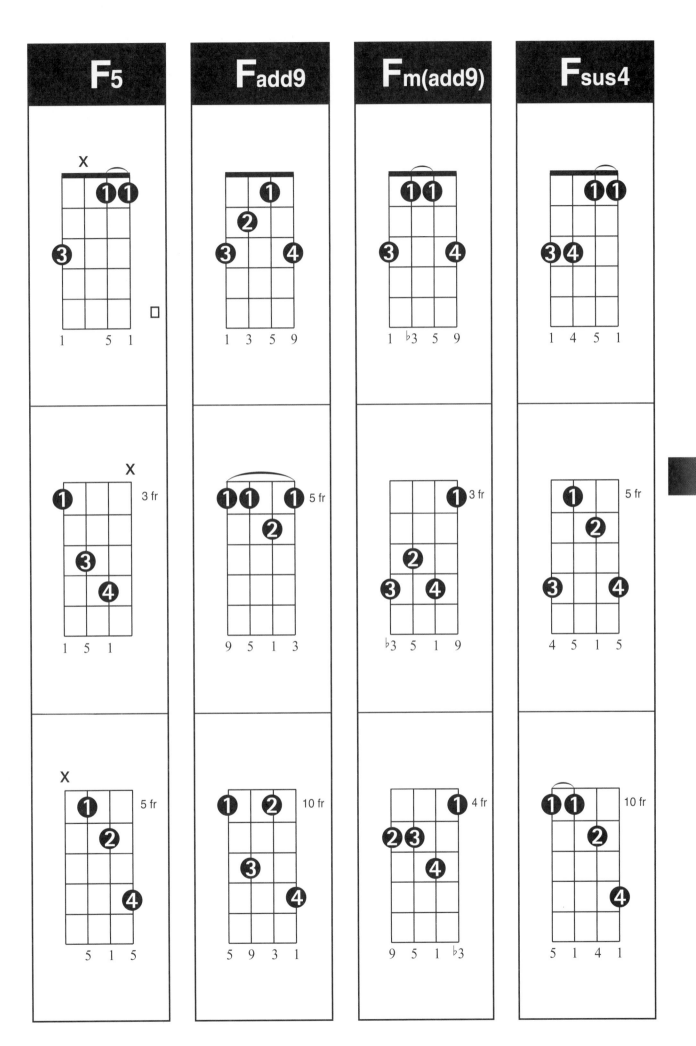

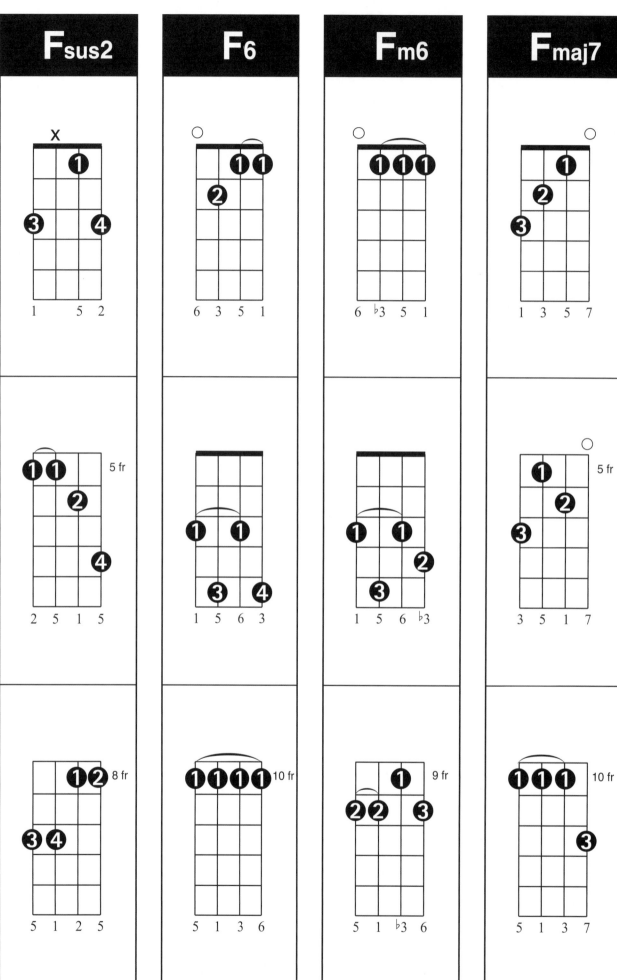

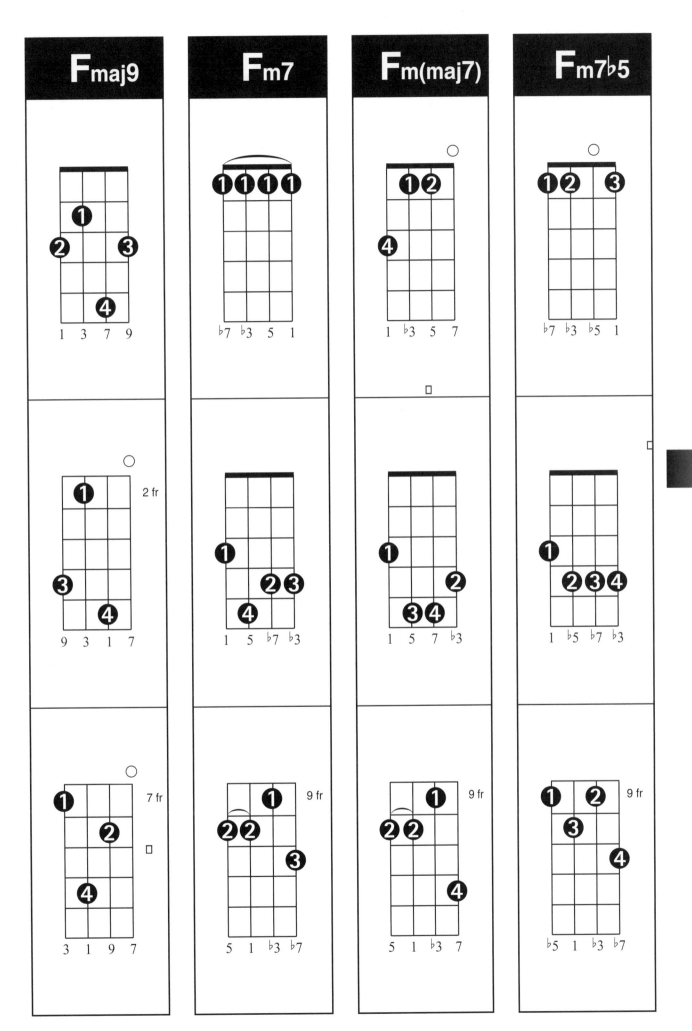

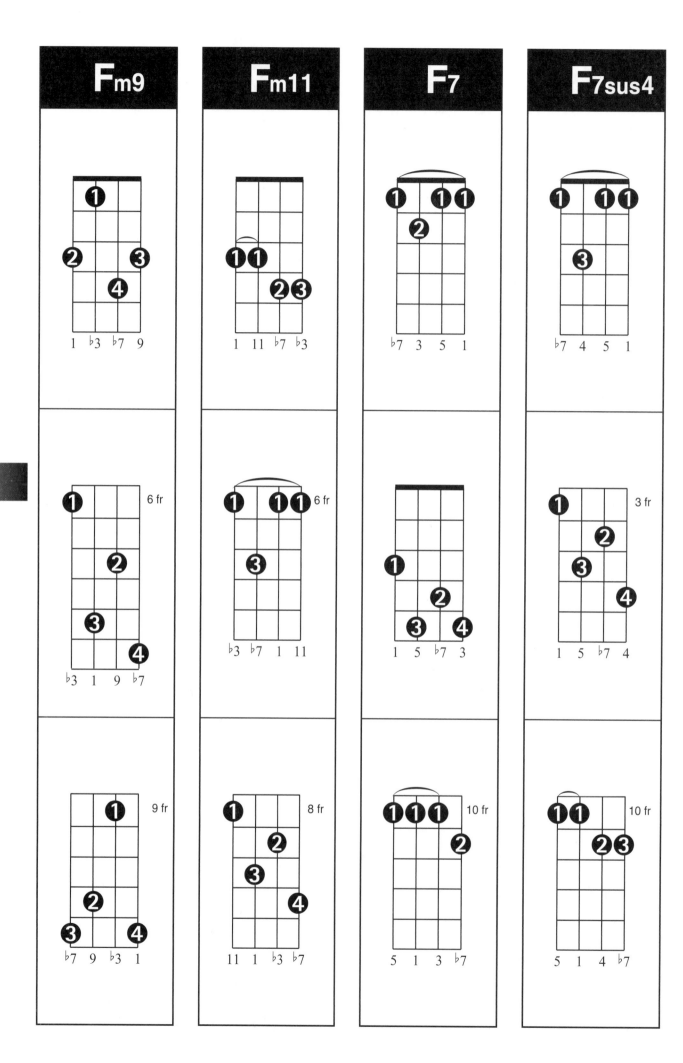

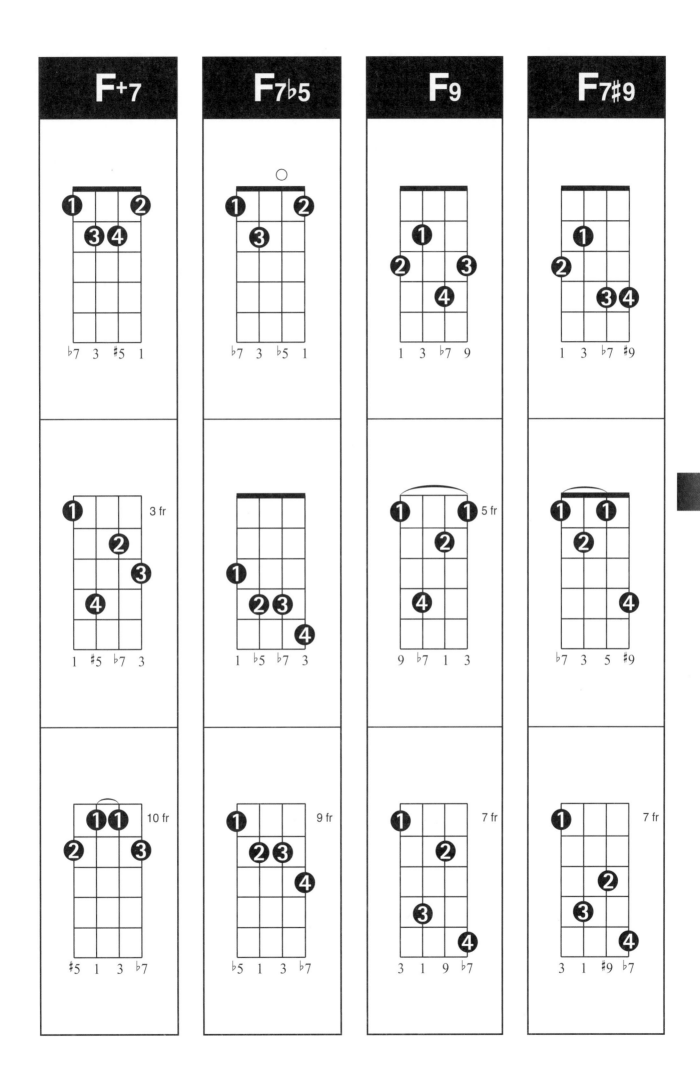

F

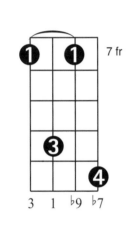
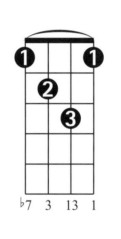
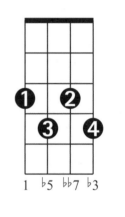

F7♭9 | F11 | F13 | F°7

F7♭9

1   3   ♭7   ♭9.

7 fr

3   1   ♭9   ♭7

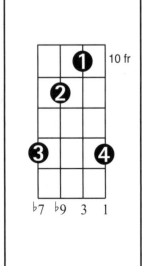

10 fr

♭7   ♭9   3   1

F11

1   11   ♭7   9

6 fr

11   ♭7   1   5

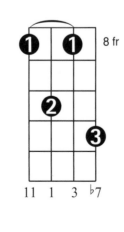

8 fr

11   1   3   ♭7

F13

13   3   ♭7   1

♭7   3   13   1

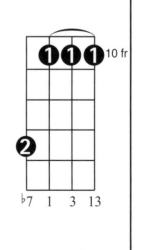

10 fr

♭7   1   3   13

F°7

♭♭7   ♭3   ♭5   1

1   ♭5   ♭♭7   ♭3

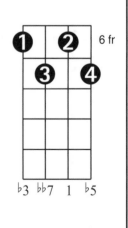

6 fr

♭3   ♭♭7   1   ♭5

F

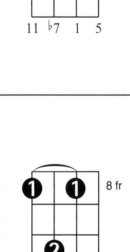

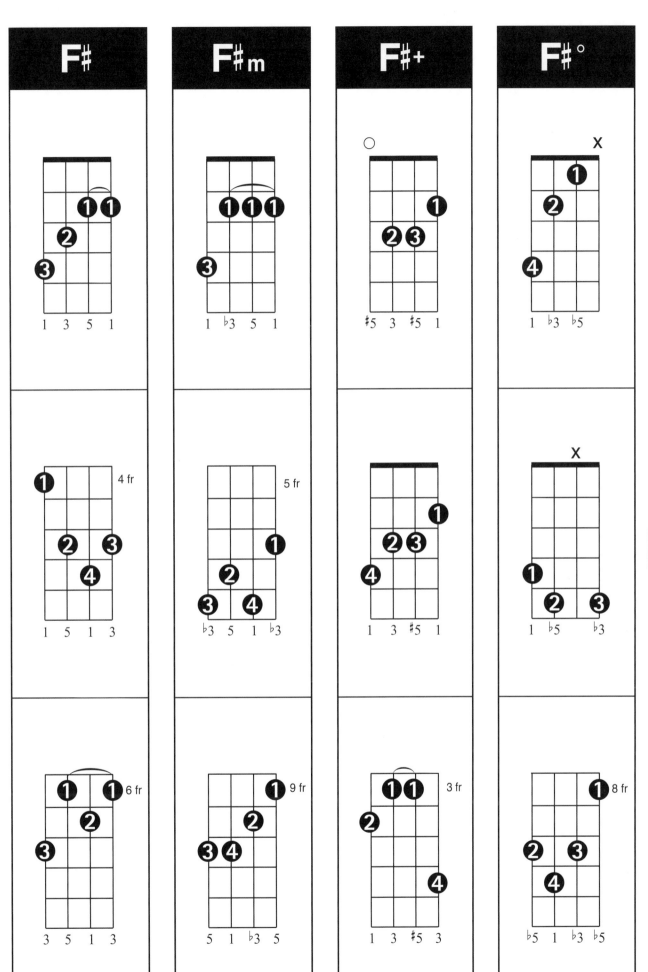

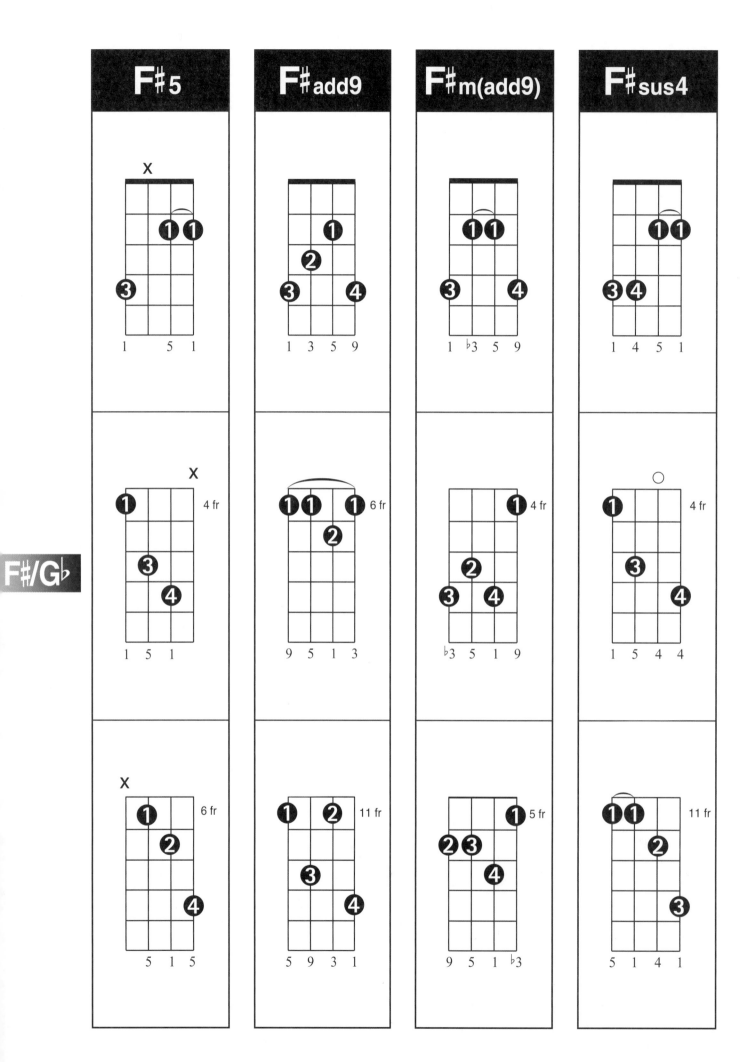

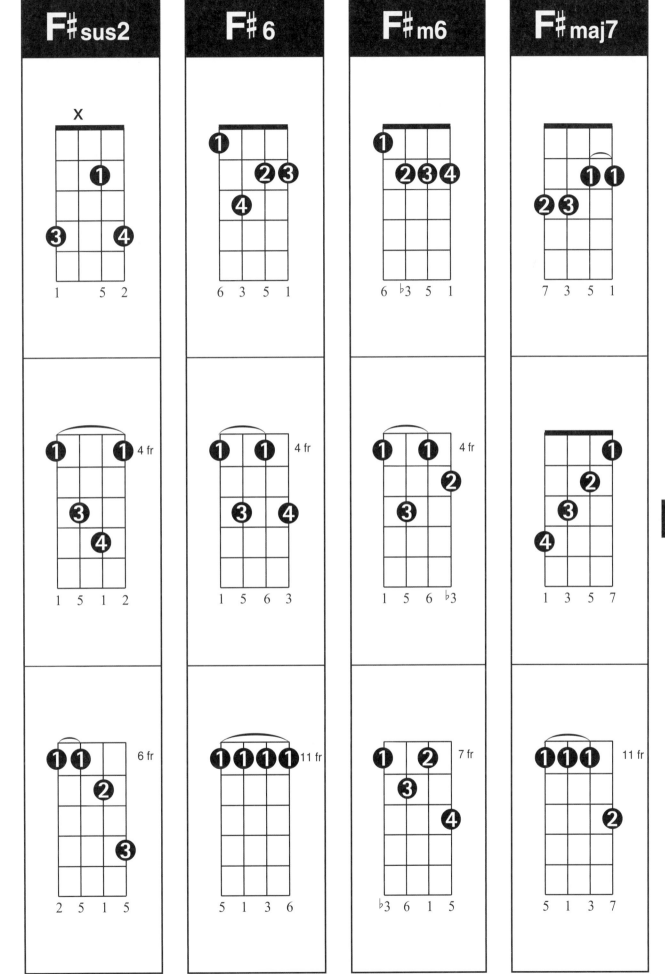

53

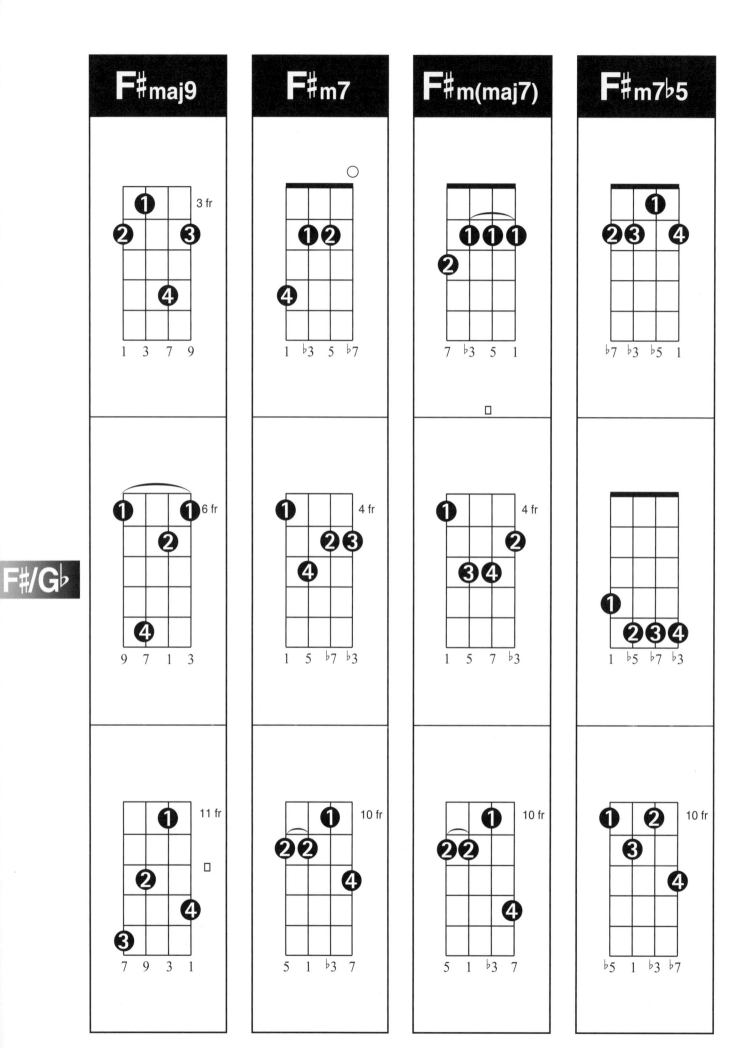

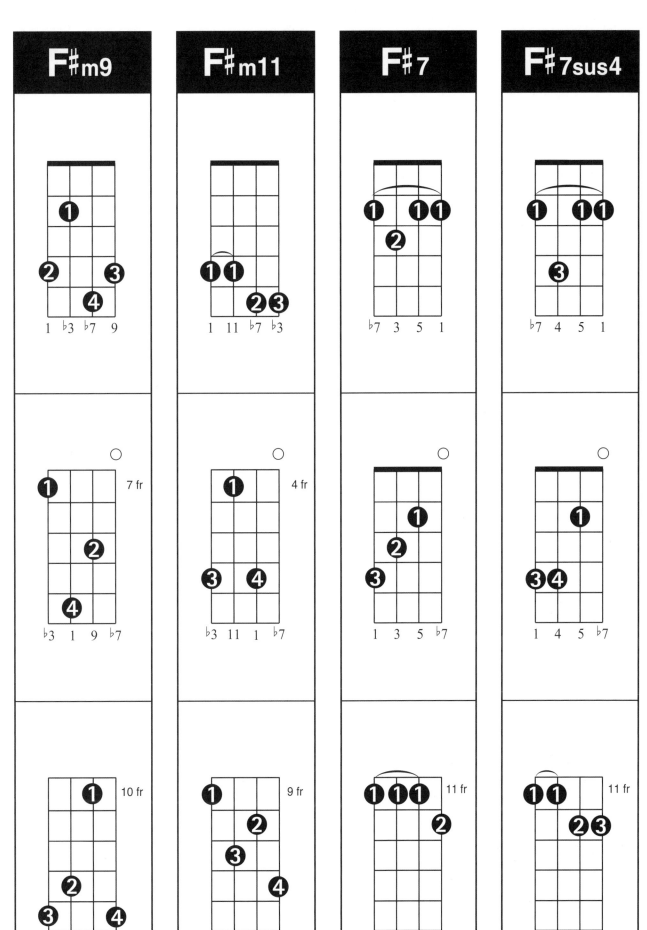

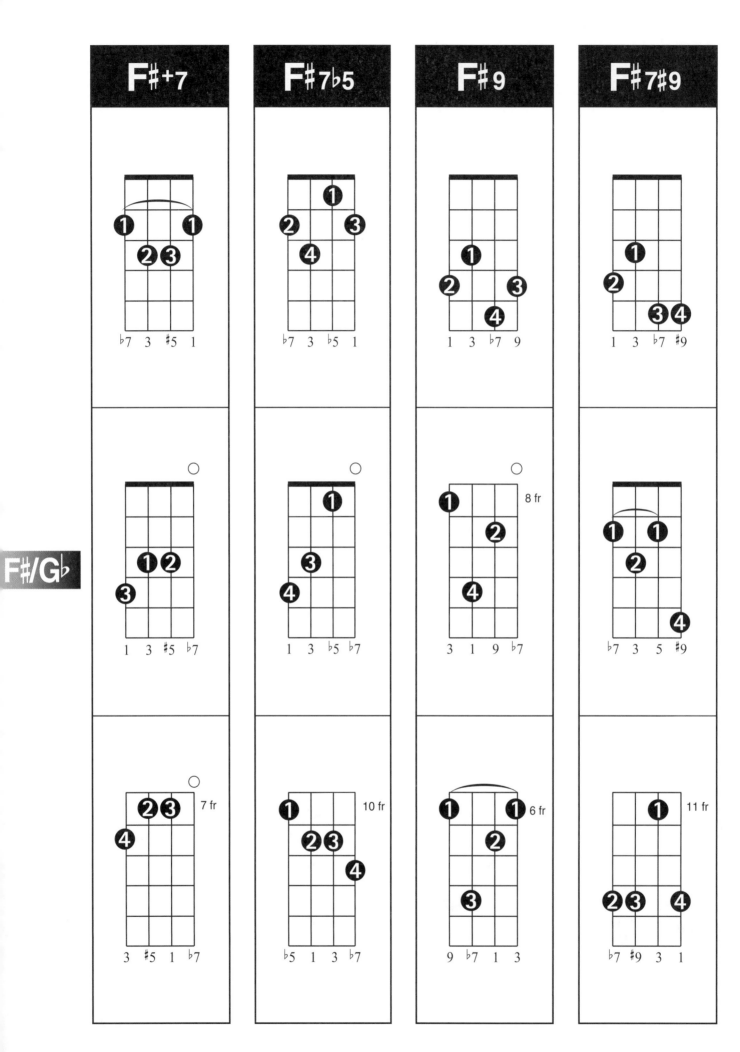

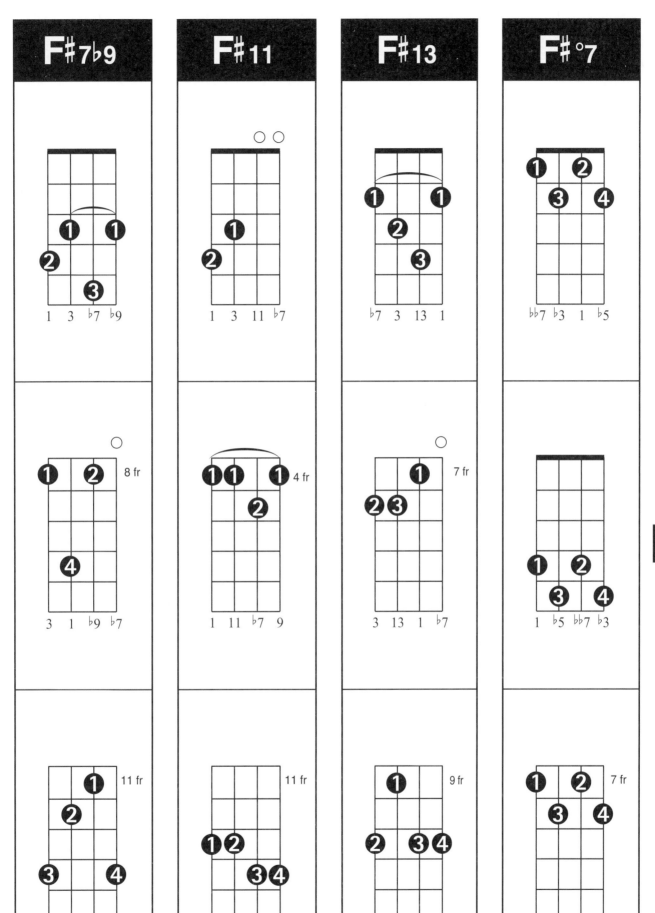

G   Gm   G+   G°

G

○ ○ ○

❸

5 1 3 1

Gm

○

❶❶❶

5 ♭3 5 1

G+

○ ○

❶

❹

♯5 1 3 1

G°

❶

❷ ❸

❹

1 ♭3 ♭5 1

G

❶❶ 3 fr

❷

❸

1 3 5 1

Gm

❶❶❶ 3 fr

❸

1 ♭3 5 1

G+

❶ 3 fr

❷❸

❹

1 3 ♯5 1

G°

❶ 5 fr

❷ ❸

❹

1 ♭5 1 ♭3

G

❶ ❶ 7 fr

❷

❸

3 5 1 3

Gm

❶ 6 fr

❷

❸ ❹

♭3 5 1 ♭3

G+

❶ 5 fr

❷

❹❸

1 ♯5 1 3

G°

❶ ❷ 6 fr

❸ ❹

♭3 ♭5 1 ♭3

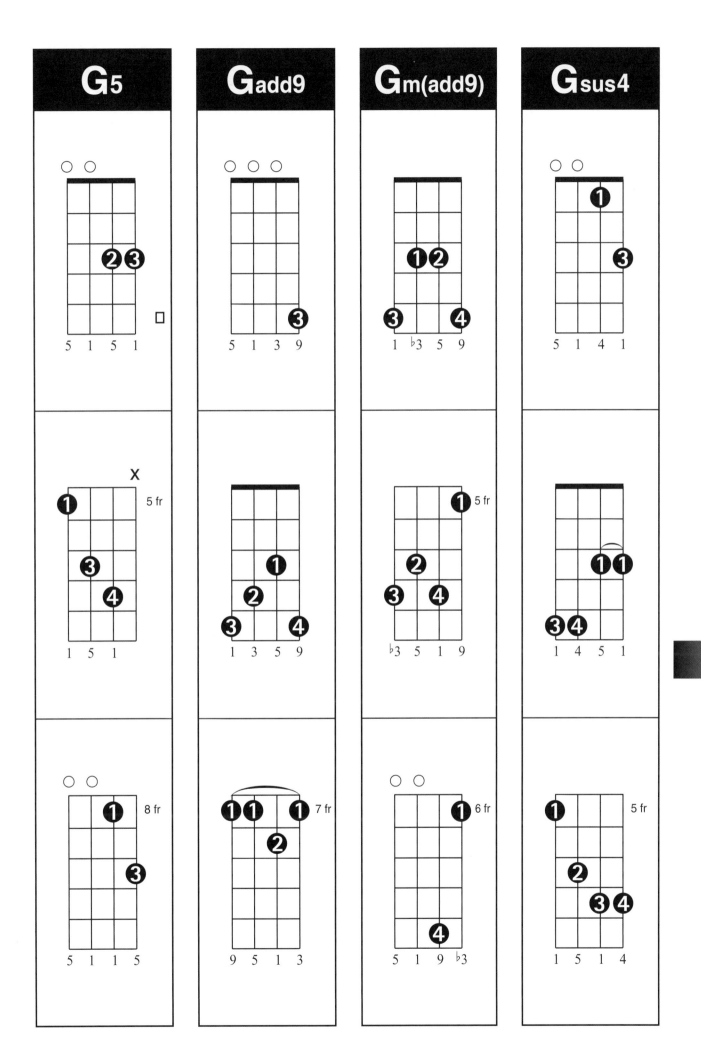

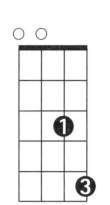
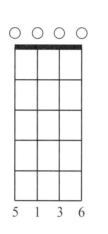
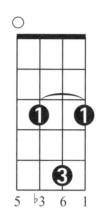
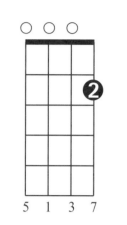

Gsus2

| 5 | 1 | 5 | 2 |

G6

| 5 | 1 | 3 | 6 |

Gm6

| 5 | ♭3 | 6 | 1 |

Gmaj7

| 5 | 1 | 3 | 7 |

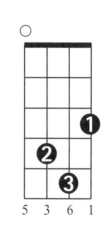
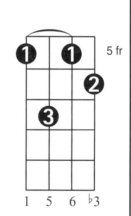
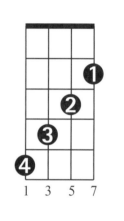

5 fr

| 1 | 5 | 1 | 2 |

5 fr

| 5 | 3 | 6 | 1 |

5 fr

| 1 | 5 | 6 | ♭3 |

5 fr

| 1 | 3 | 5 | 7 |

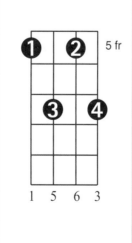
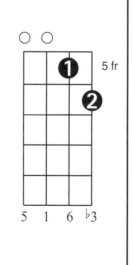
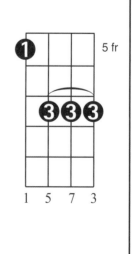

7 fr

| 2 | 5 | 1 | 5 |

5 fr

| 1 | 5 | 6 | 3 |

5 fr

| 5 | 1 | 6 | ♭3 |

5 fr

| 1 | 5 | 7 | 3 |

G

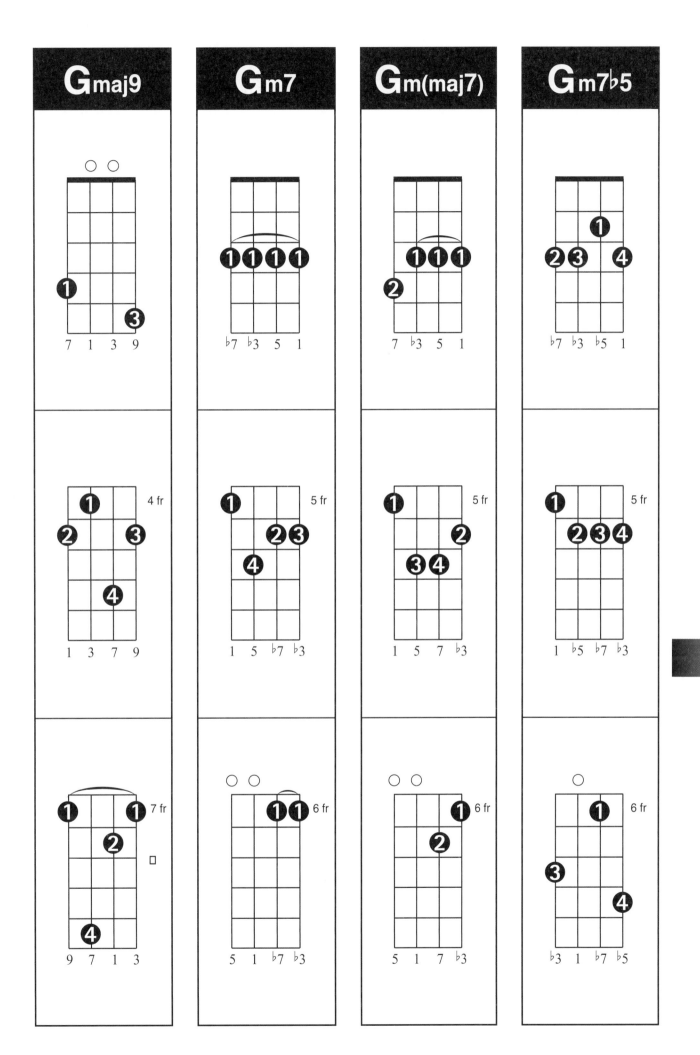

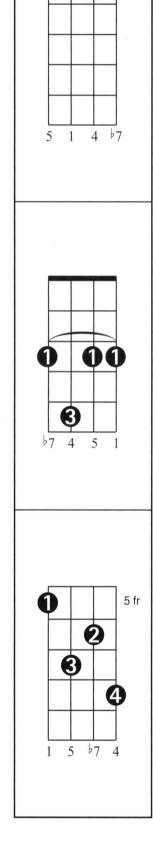

Gm9   Gm11   G7   G7sus4

Gm9

3 fr

1 ♭3 ♭7 9

5 fr

♭3 1 ♭7 9

6 fr

9 1 ♭7 ♭3

Gm11

♭7 ♭3 11 1

5 fr

1 11 ♭7 ♭3

6 fr

♭3 1 ♭9 11

G7

5 1 3 ♭7

♭7 3 5 1

5 fr

1 5 ♭7 3

G7sus4

5 1 4 ♭7

♭7 4 5 1

5 fr

1 5 ♭7 4

G

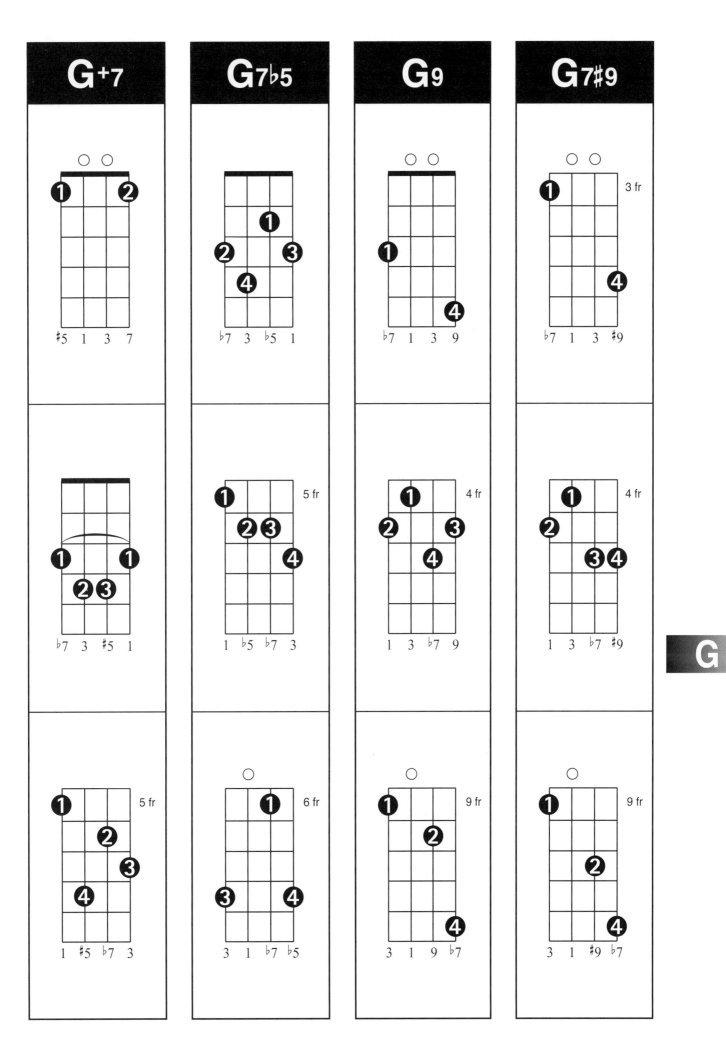

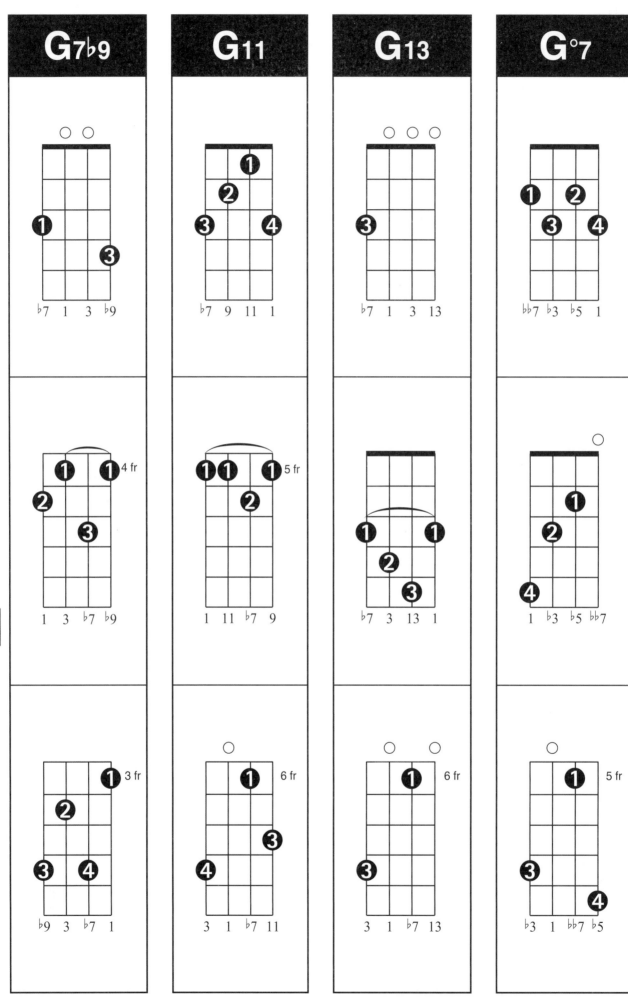

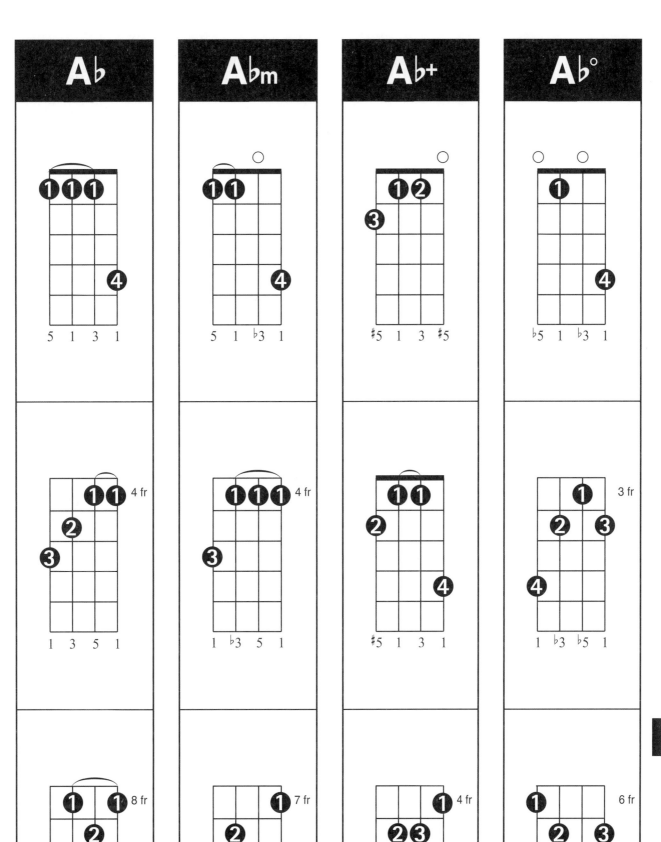

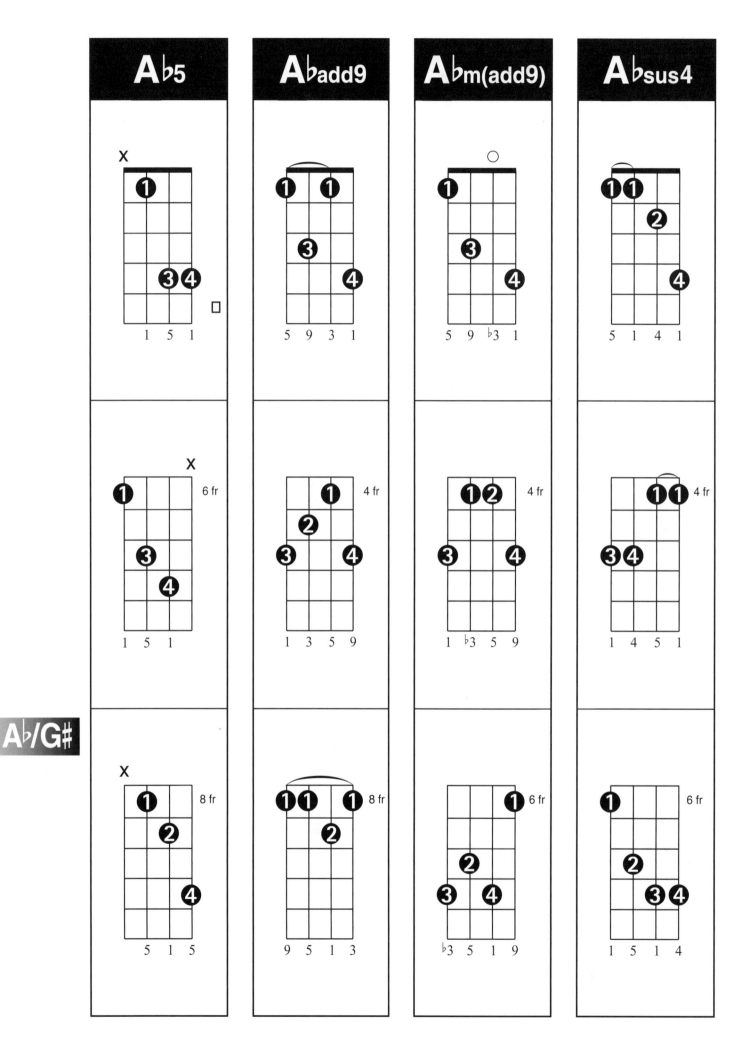

Absus2

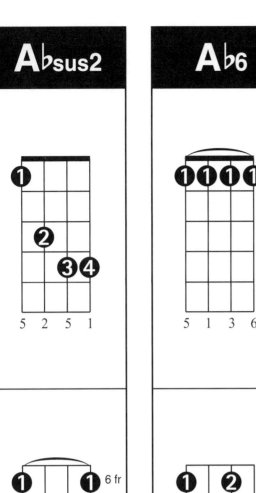

5 2 5 1

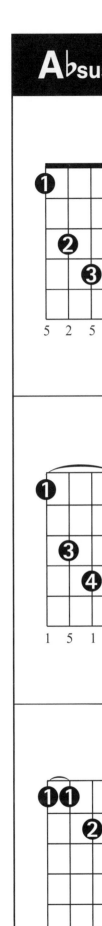

1 5 1 2

1 1 · 8 fr

2

4

2 5 1 5

Ab6

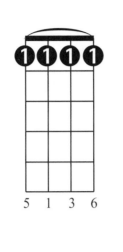

5 1 3 6

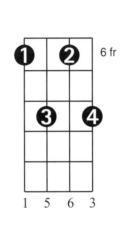

1 5 6 3

· 9 fr

3 6 1 5

Abm6

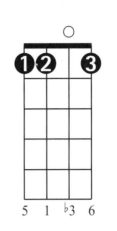

5 1 b3 6

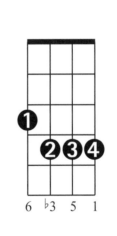

6 b3 5 1

· 6 fr

1 5 6 b3

Abmaj7

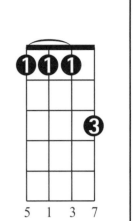

5 1 3 7

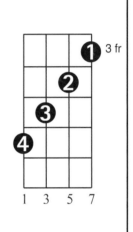

1 3 5 7

· 6 fr

1 5 7 3

Ab/G#

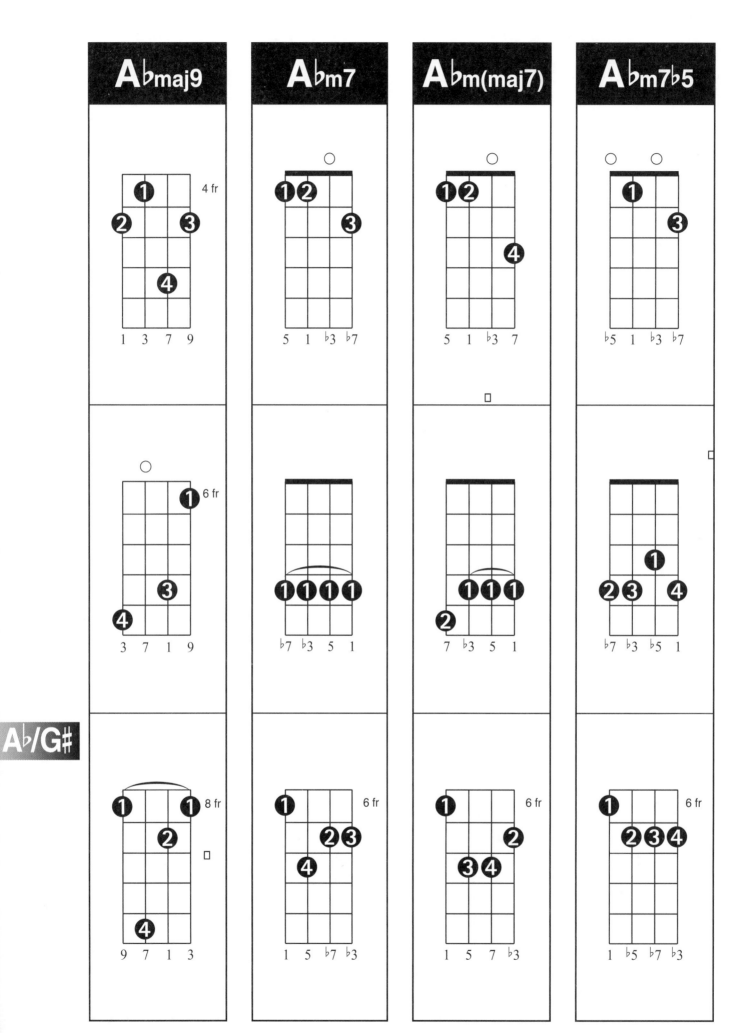

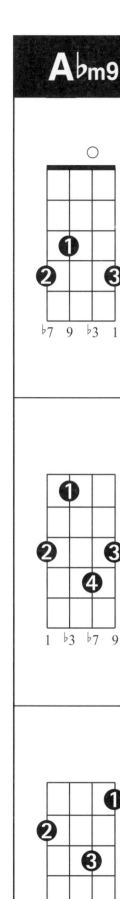
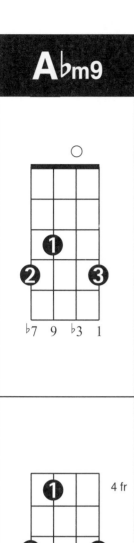
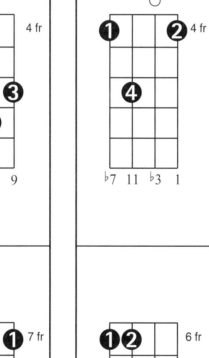
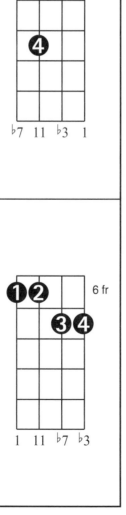

A♭m9

| ♭7 | 9 | ♭3 | 1 |

4 fr

| 1 | ♭3 | ♭7 | 9 |

7 fr

| 9 | ♭7 | 1 | ♭3 |

A♭m11

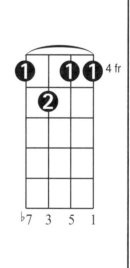
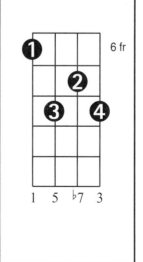

| ♭7 | ♭3 | 11 | 1 |

4 fr

| ♭7 | 11 | ♭3 | 1 |

6 fr

| 1 | 11 | ♭7 | ♭3 |

A♭7

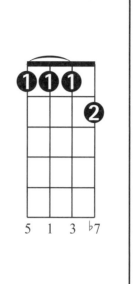
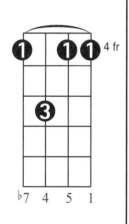

| 5 | 1 | 3 | ♭7 |

4 fr

| ♭7 | 3 | 5 | 1 |

6 fr

| 1 | 5 | ♭7 | 3 |

A♭7sus4

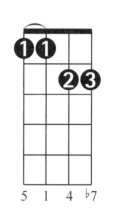
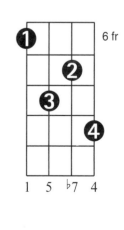

| 5 | 1 | 4 | ♭7 |

4 fr

| ♭7 | 4 | 5 | 1 |

6 fr

| 1 | 5 | ♭7 | 4 |

A♭/G#

69

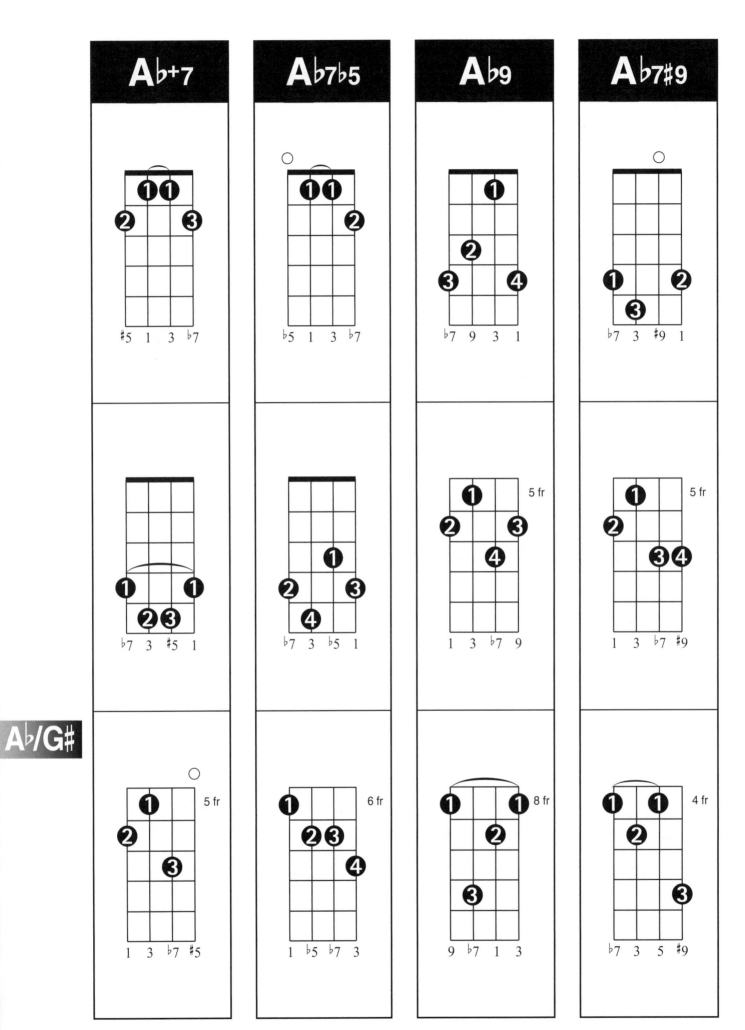

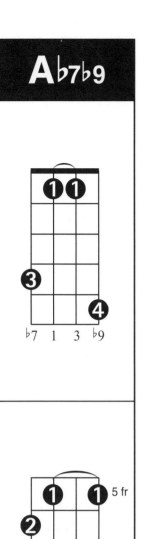

A♭7♭9

♭7   1   3   ♭9

1   3   ♭7   ♭9   5 fr

♭9   ♭7   1   3   7 fr

A♭11

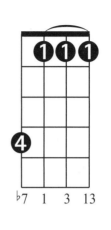

♭7   9   11   1

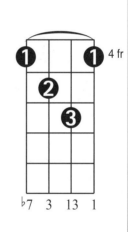

1   11   ♭7   9   6 fr

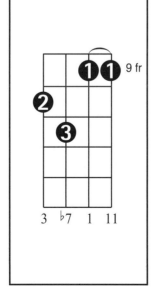

3   ♭7   1   11   9 fr

A♭13

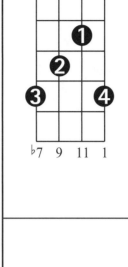

♭7   1   3   13

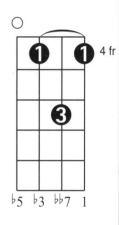

♭7   3   13   1   4 fr

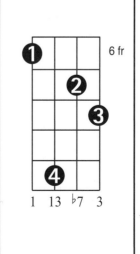

1   13   ♭7   3   6 fr

A♭°7

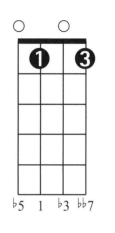

♭5   1   ♭3   ♭♭7

♭5   ♭3   ♭♭7   1   4 fr

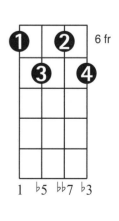

1   ♭5   ♭♭7   ♭3   6 fr

A♭/G#

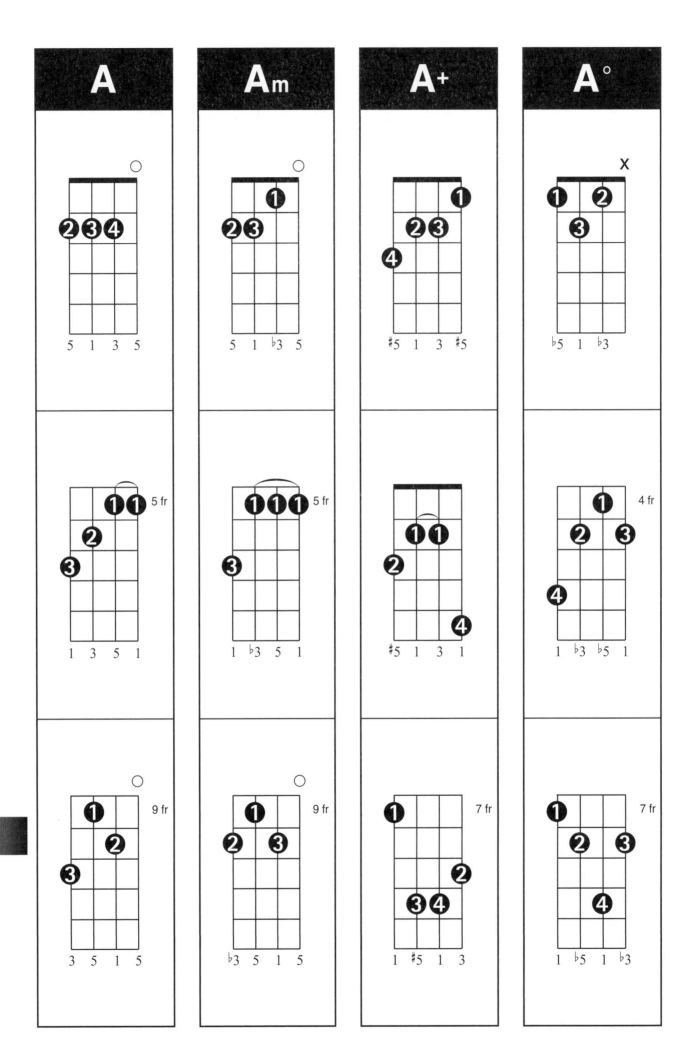

A

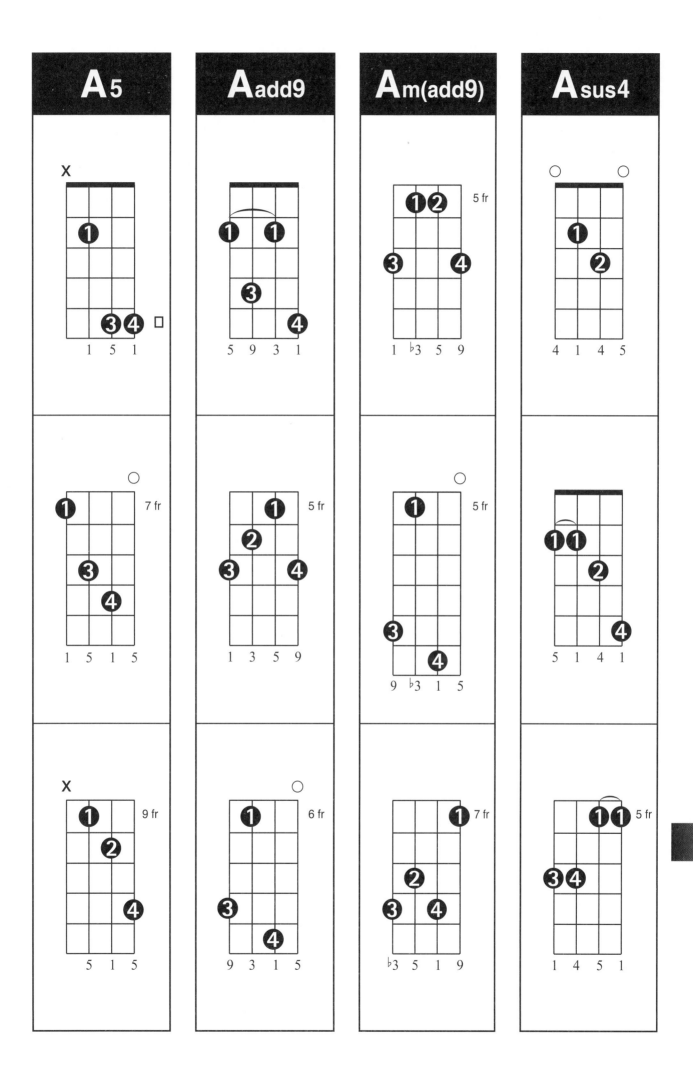

Asus2   A6   Am6   Amaj7

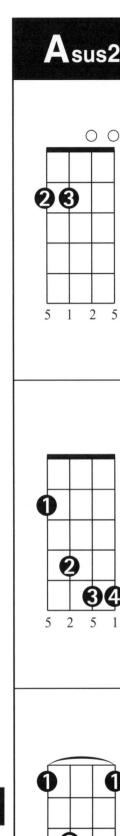
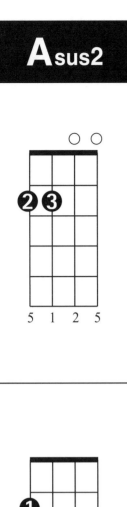

Asus2

○ ○

❷ ❸

5 1 2 5

❶

❷

❸ ❹

5 2 5 1

❶   ❶ 7 fr

❷

❸

1 5 1 2

A6

○

❶ ❷

❹

6 1 3 5

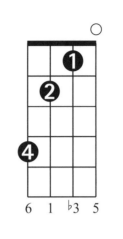

❶ ❶ ❶ ❶

5 1 3 6

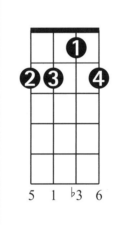

❶ ❷ 7 fr

❸ ❹

1 5 6 3

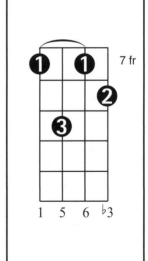

Am6

○

❶

❷

❹

6 1 ♭3 5

❶

❷❸   ❹

5 1 ♭3 6

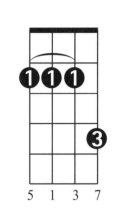

❶ ❶ 7 fr

❷

❸

1 5 6 ♭3

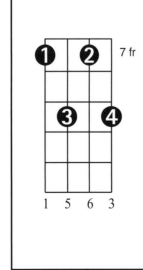

Amaj7

○

❶ ❶ ❶

❸

5 1 3 7

❶ 4 fr

❷

❸

❹

1 3 5 7

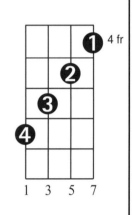

○

❶ 6 fr

❷

❹

1 3 7 5

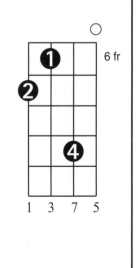

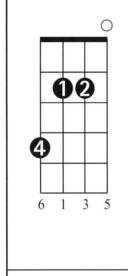
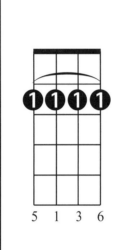

74

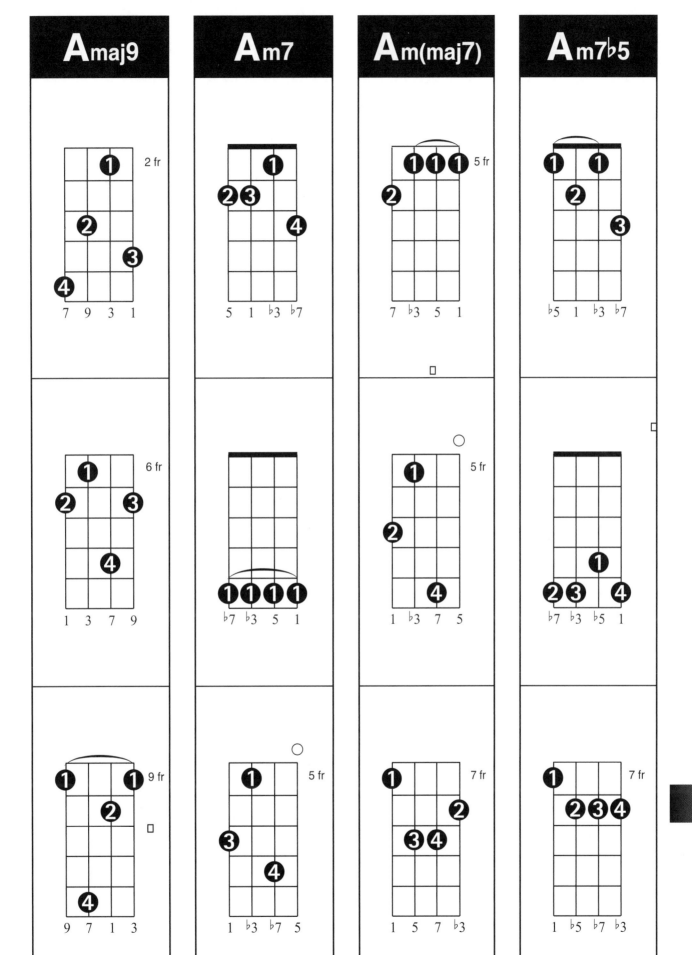

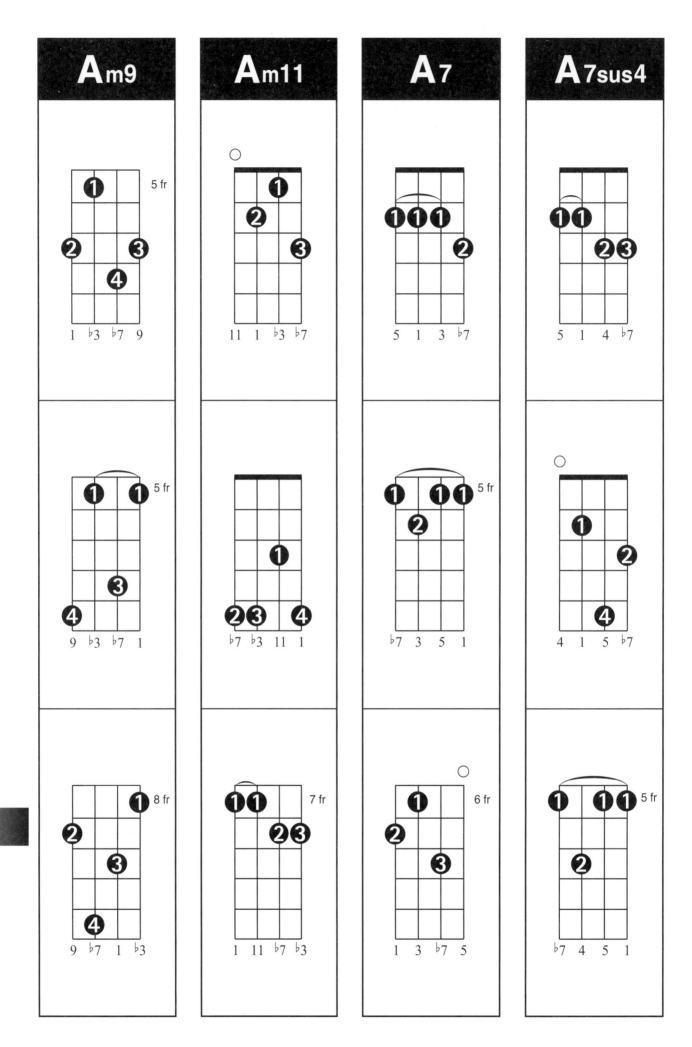

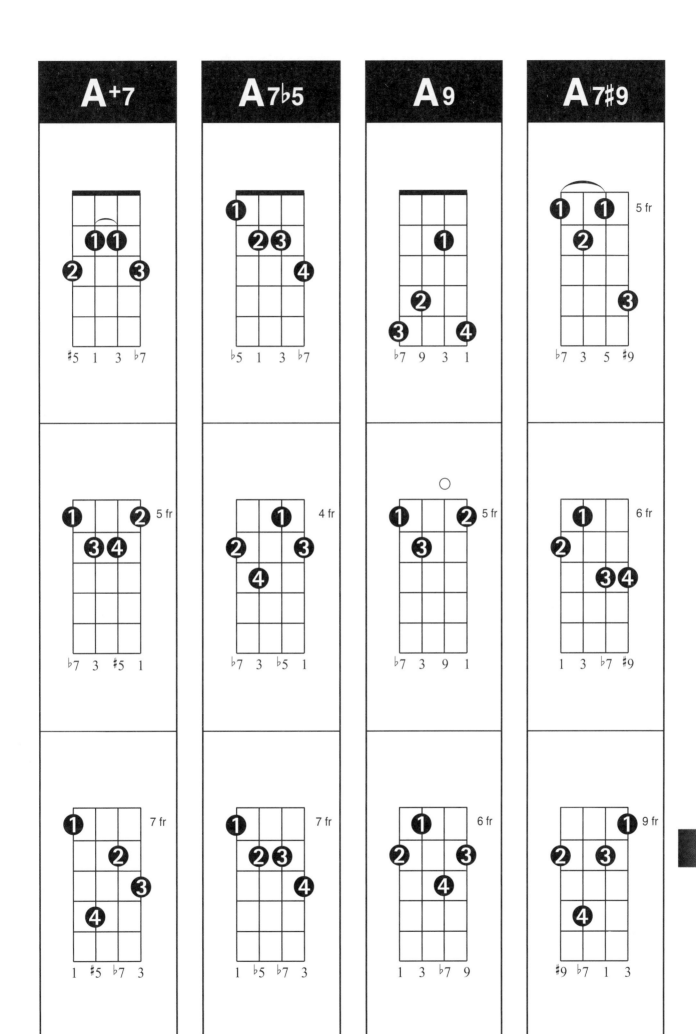

A7♭9

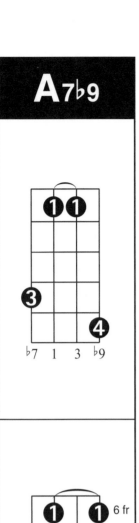

♭7 1 3 ♭9

1 3 ♭7 ♭9   6 fr

♭9 ♭7 1 3   8 fr

A11

5 1 11 ♭7

♭7 3 11 1   3 fr

1 11 ♭7 9   7 fr

A13

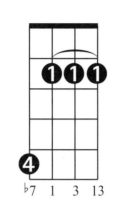

♭7 1 3 13

13 1 3 ♭7

♭7 3 13 1   5 fr

A°7

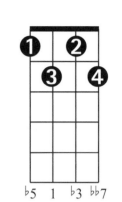

♭5 1 ♭3 ♭♭7

♭♭7 ♭3 ♭5 1

1 ♭5 ♭♭7 ♭3   7 fr

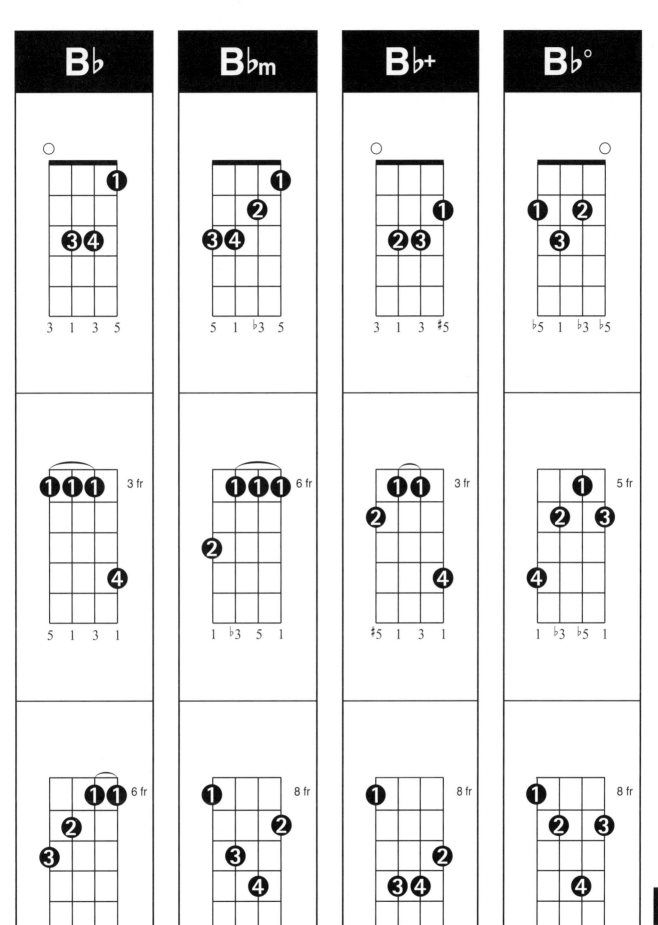

B♭/A♯

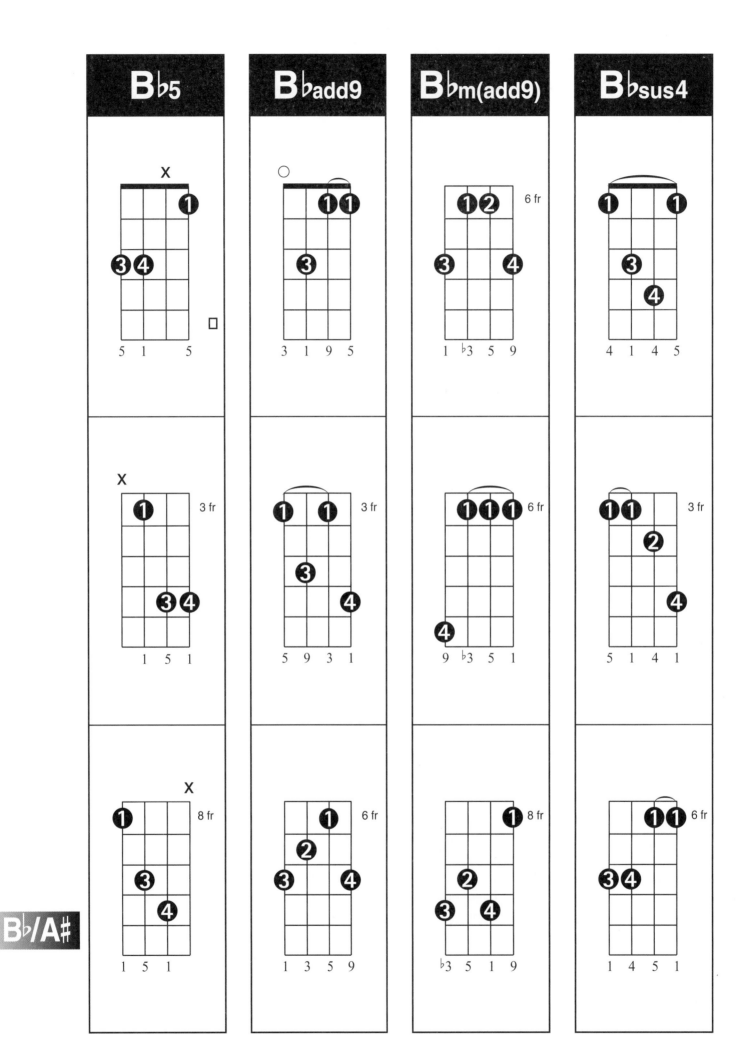

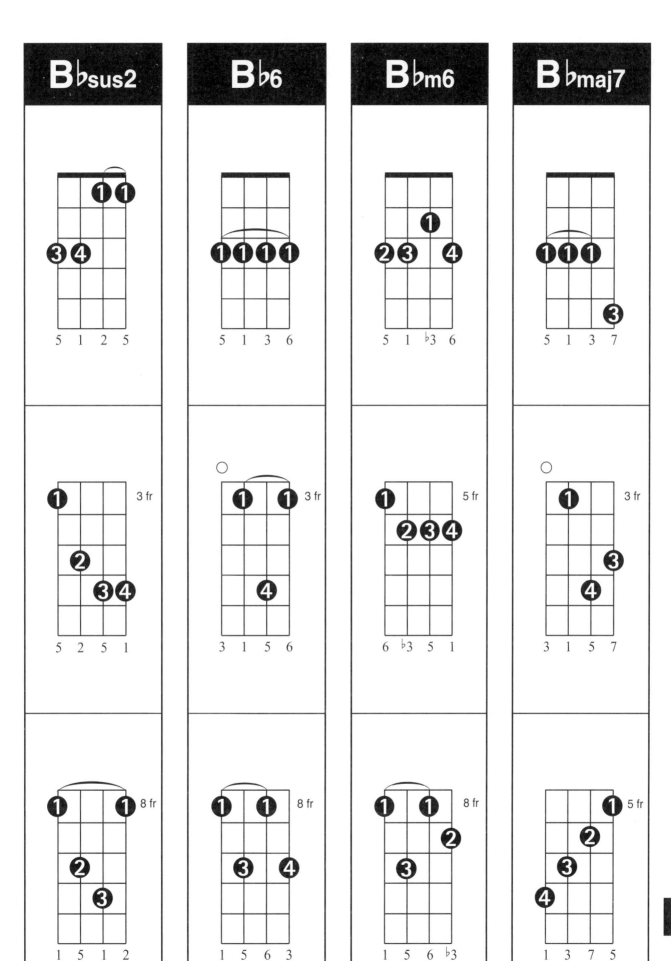

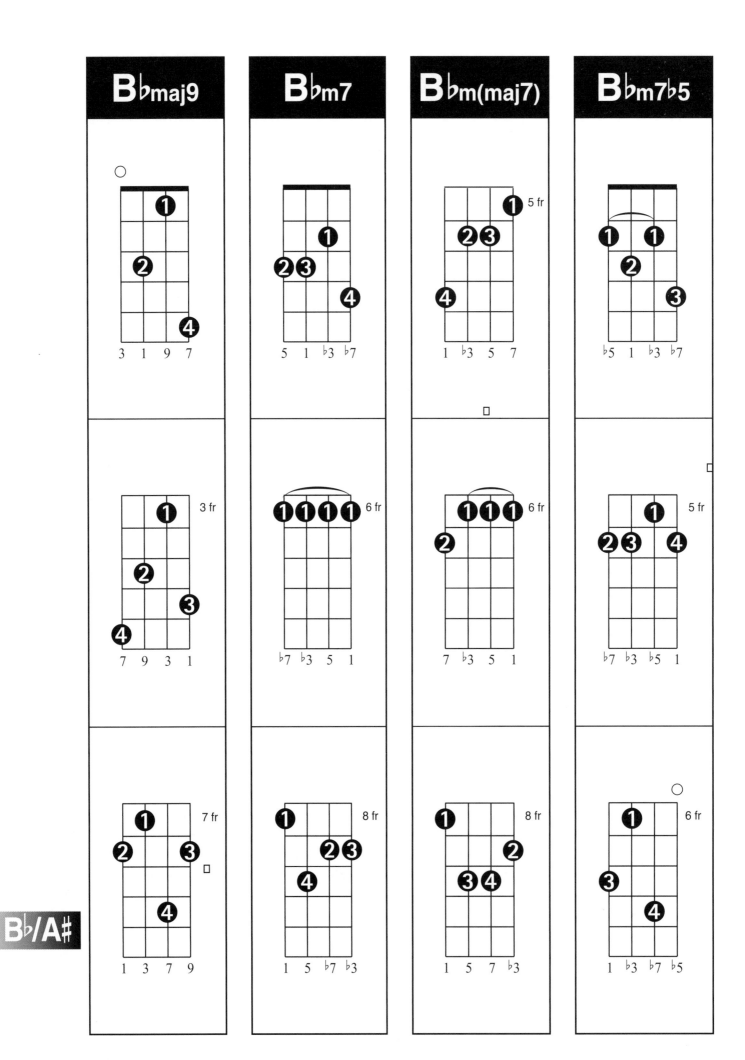

B♭maj9   B♭m7   B♭m(maj7)   B♭m7♭5

B♭/A♯

82

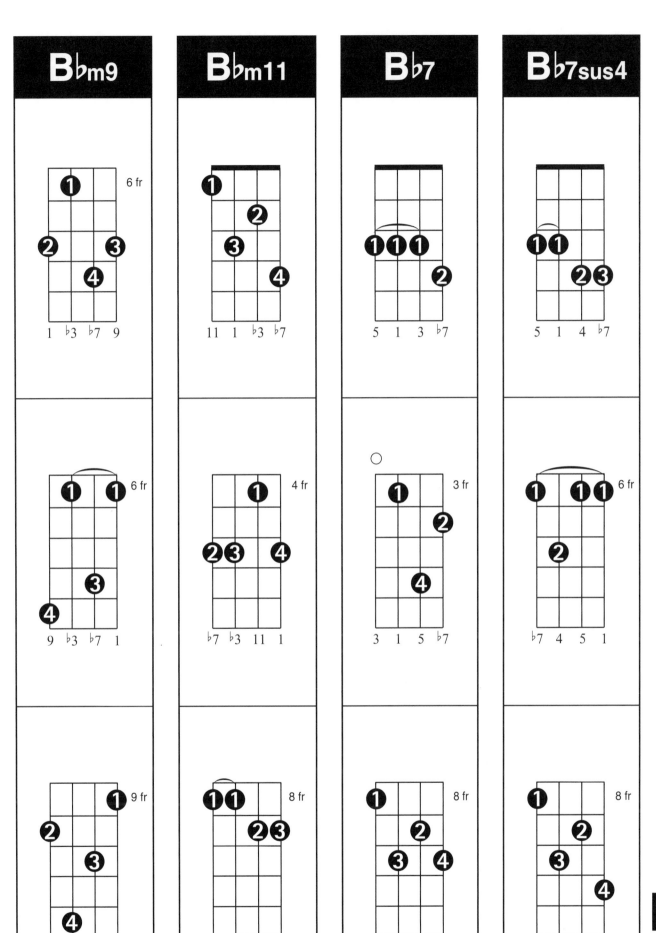

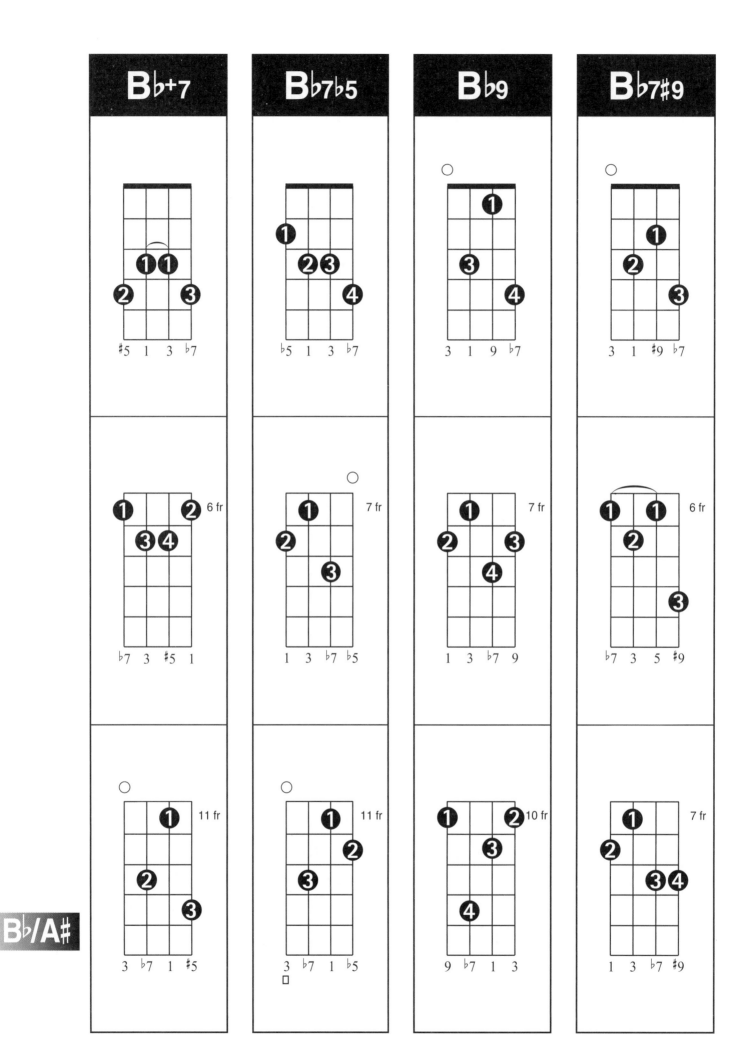

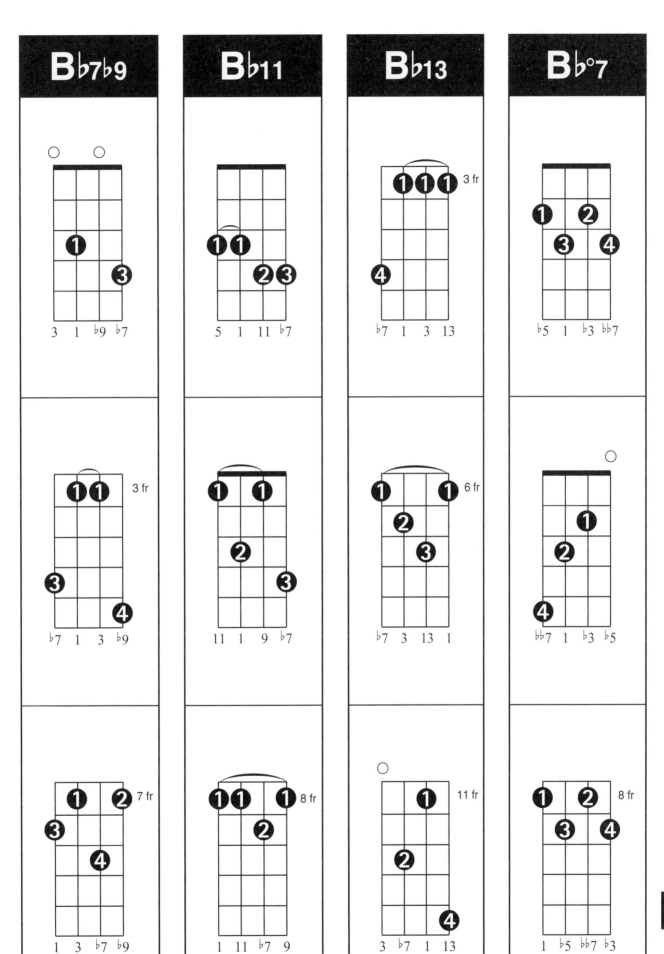

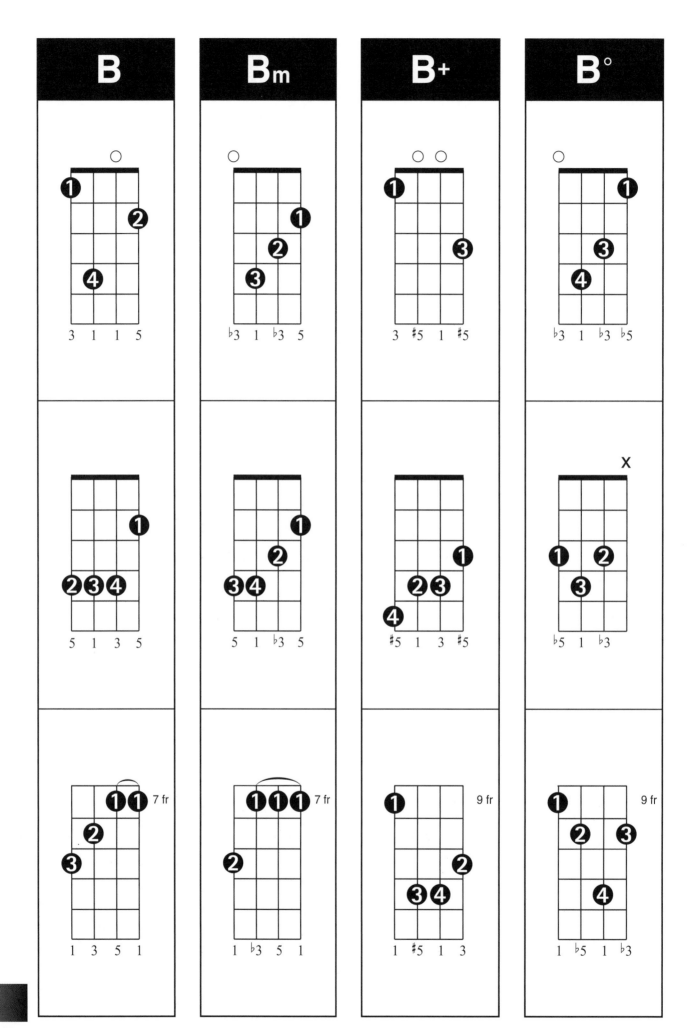

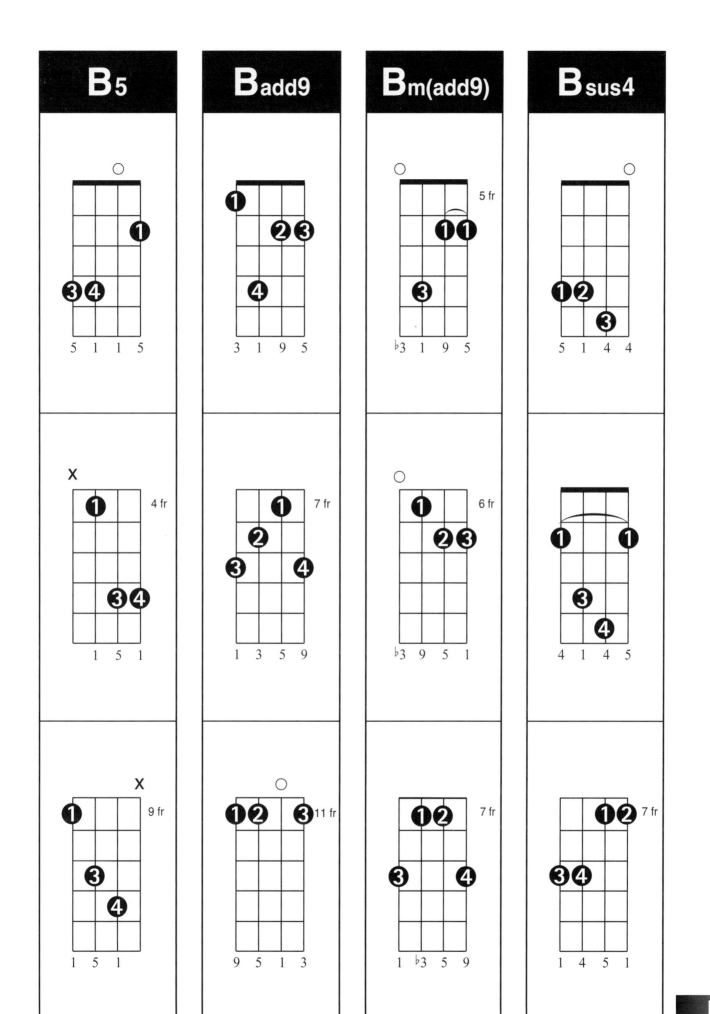

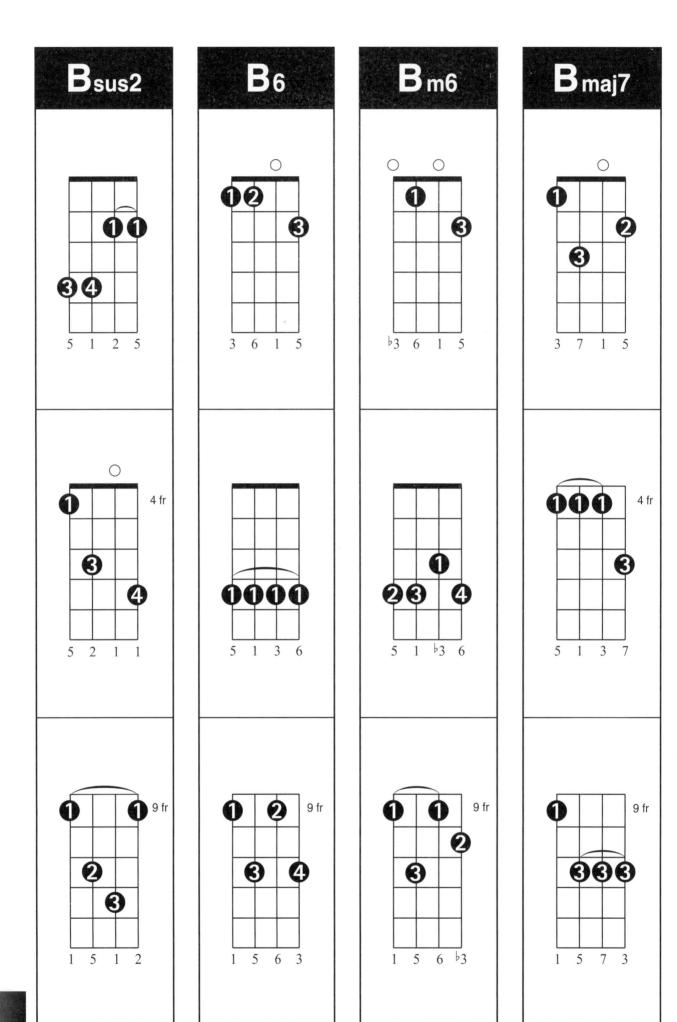

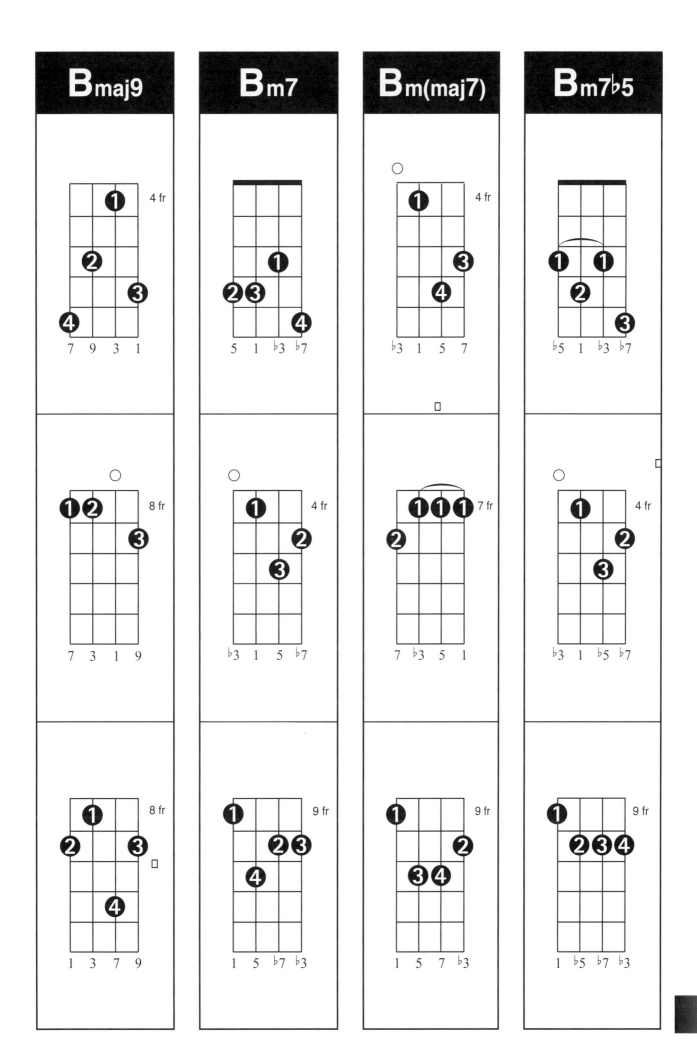

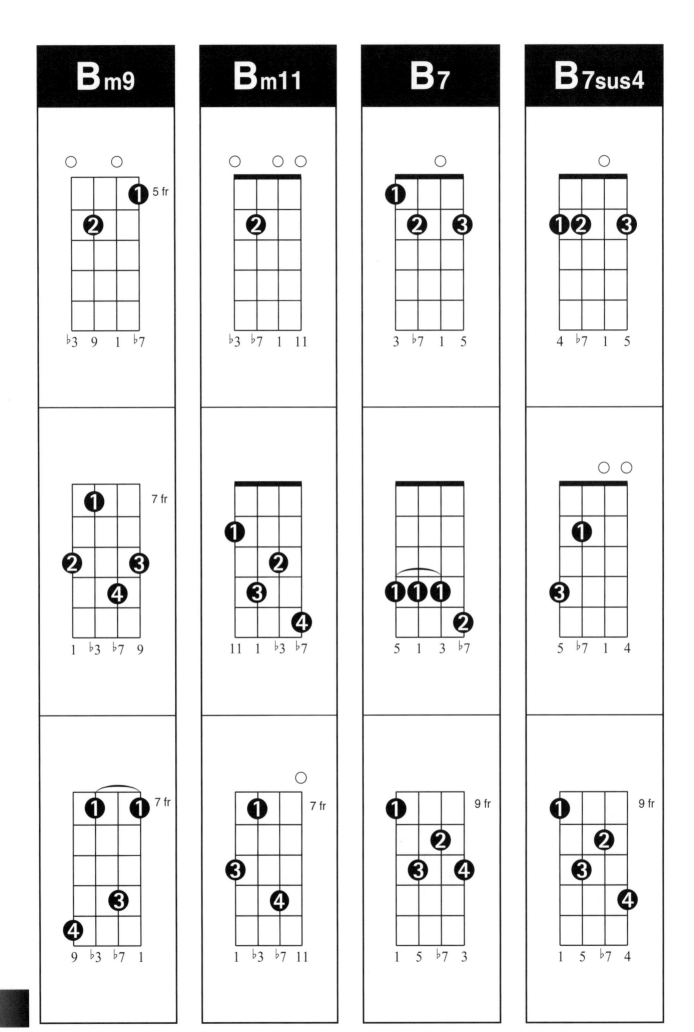

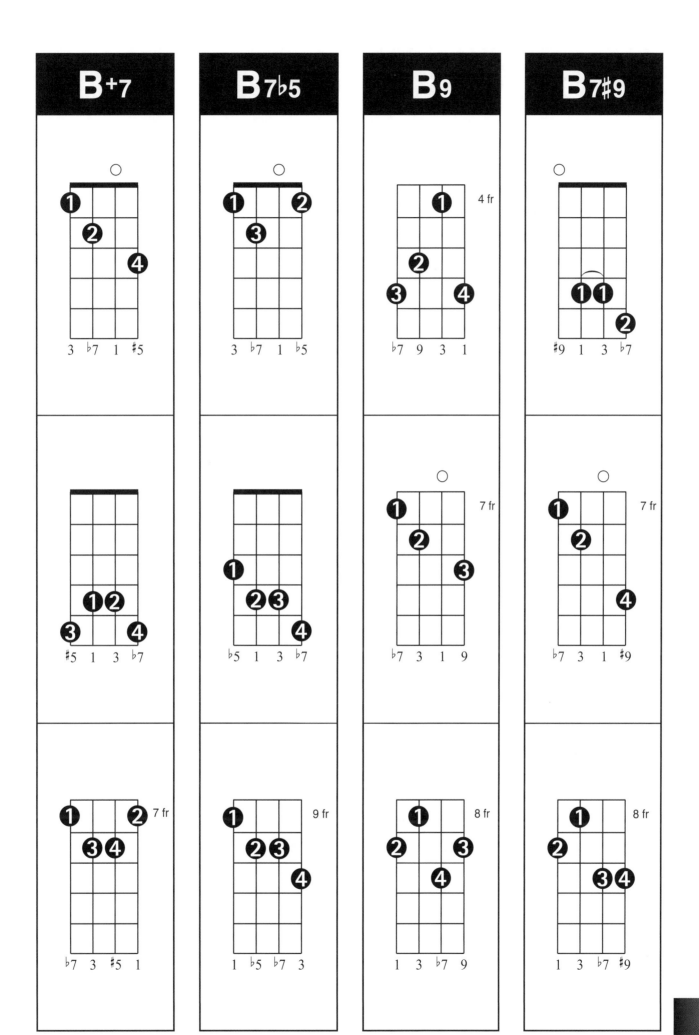

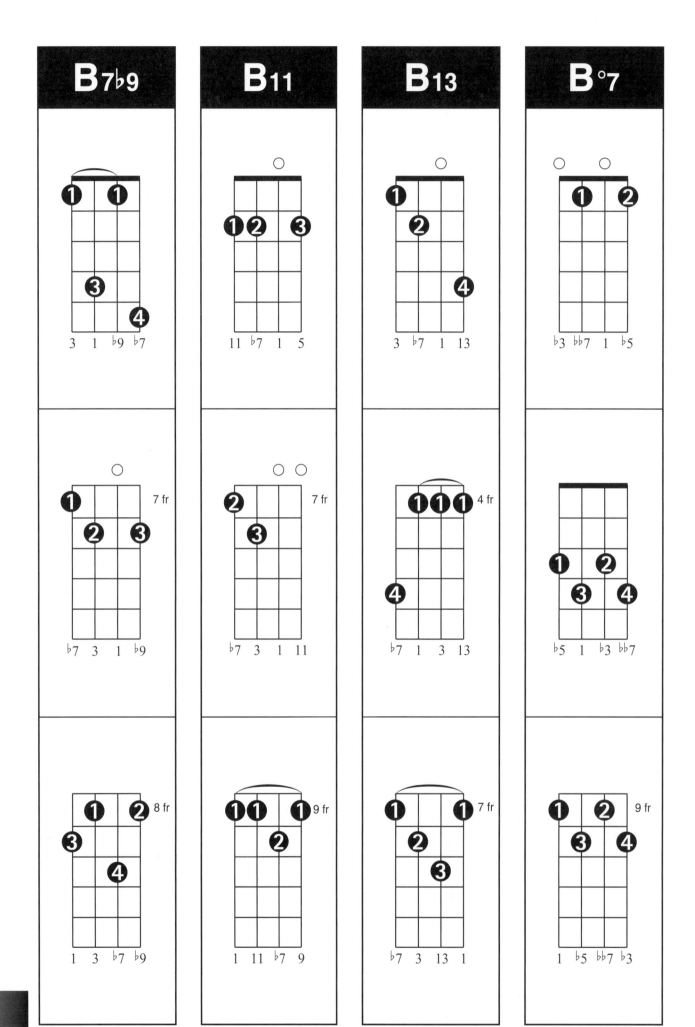

Learn to play the
Ukulele
with these great Hal Leonard books!

Hal Leonard Ukulele Method

Book 1
by Lil' Rev

The Hal Leonard Ukulele Method is designed for anyone just learning to play ukulele. This comprehensive and easy-to-use beginner's guide by acclaimed performer and uke master Lil' Rev includes many fun songs of different styles to learn and play. The accompanying audio contains 46 tracks of songs for demonstration and play along. Includes: types of ukuleles, tuning, music reading, melody playing, chords, strumming, scales, tremolo, music notation and tablature, a variety of music styles, ukulele history and much more.

00695847 Book Only $8.99
00695832 Book/Online Audio $12.99
00320534 DVD $14.99

Book 2
00695948 Book Only $7.99
00695949 Book/Online Audio $11.99

Ukulele Chord Finder
00695803 9" x 12"... $8.99
00695902 6" x 9"... $7.99
00696472 Book 1 with Online Audio + Chord Finder $16.99

Ukulele Scale Finder
00696378 9" x 12"... $8.99

Easy Songs for Ukulele
00695904 Book/Online Audio $16.99
00695905 Book... $9.99

Ukulele for Kids
00696468 Book/Online Audio $14.99
00244855 Method & Songbook $22.99

Baritone Ukulele Method – Book 1
00696564 Book/Online Audio $12.99

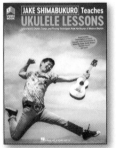

Jake Shimabukuro Teaches Ukulele Lessons
Learn notes, chords, songs, and playing techniques from the master of modern ukulele! In this unique book with online video, Jake Shimabukuro will get you started on playing the ukulele. The book includes full transcriptions of every example, the video features Jake teaching you everything you need to know plus video of Jake playing all the examples.
00320992 Book/Online Video $22.99

Ukulele Aerobics
For All Levels, from Beginner to Advanced
by Chad Johnson
This package provides practice material for every day of the week and includes an online audio access code for all the workouts in the book. Techniques covered include: strumming, fingerstyle, slides, bending, damping, vibrato, tremolo and more.
00102162 Book/Online Audio $19.99

Fretboard Roadmaps – Ukulele
The Essential Patterns That All the Pros Know and Use
by Fred Sokolow & Jim Beloff
Take your uke playing to the next level! Tunes and exercises in standard notation and tab illustrate each technique. Absolute beginners can follow the diagrams and instruction step-by-step, while intermediate and advanced players can use the chapters non-sequentially to increase their understanding of the ukulele. The audio includes 59 demo and play-along tracks.
00695901 Book/Online Audio $15.99

All About Ukulele
A Fun and Simple Guide to Playing Ukulele
by Chad Johnson
If you wish there was a fun and engaging way to motivate you in your uke playing quest, then this is it: All About Ukulele is for you. Whether it's learning to read music, playing in a band, finding the right instrument, or all of the above, this enjoyable guide will help you.
00233655 Book/Online Audio $19.99

Play Ukulele Today!
A Complete Guide to the Basics
by Barrett Tagliarino
This is the ultimate self-teaching method for ukulele! Includes audio with full demo tracks and over 60 great songs. You'll learn: care for the instrument; how to produce sound; reading music notation and rhythms; and more.
00699638 Book/Online Audio.................................. $12.99
00293927 Book 1 & 2/Online Media......................... $19.99

HAL•LEONARD®
www.halleonard.com

Prices, contents and availability subject to change without notice. Prices listed in U.S. funds.